LETTERS TO MY SISTERS

~ The Fearless Storytellers ~

Copyright © 2022 by Adrienne E. Bell and The Fearless Storytellers Movement
Printed in the United States of America
ISBN- 9798371752475

All rights reserved. No part of this publication may be reproduced, stored in a retrieval system, or transmitted in any form or by any means electronic, mechanical, photocopying, recording or otherwise –without the prior permission of the publisher. Some names and identifying details have been changed to protect the privacy of individuals.

https://www.fearlessstorytellers.com/

Cover Credit: Jatori Frazier

TABLE OF CONTENTS

Acknowledgements v
Dedication vii

A Letter to My Sisters
    Tamara P. Fields, LCSW-S 3
In My Memories (Introduction)
    Lenora Jones Elliott 5
Reclaiming My Journey
    Lenora Jones Elliott 7
The Sun Will Come Up Tomorrow
    Angela Whitfield 13
A Bag of Broken Pieces
    Aleida Salas 31
The Divine Divorce
    Sound Whisdom 49
I am the Breaker
    Lenora Jones Elliott 65
It Comes in Waves
    Nikki Duncan Talley 71
Acknowledging the Void
    Lakeisha Wilson 87
The Invisible Me
    Lenora Jones Elliott 93

You Are Not Alone! 97

ACKNOWLEDGEMENTS

Extreme thanks to my AMAZING Chief Storytelling Officer, Vernisha Parrish. The stories were elevated to the next dimension due to your attention to detail and heart to see the Storytellers portrayed with dignity, class, and grace. Thank you for your commitment to the souls of women everywhere.

Special thanks to Tamara Fields, LCSW-S, for your uplifting perspective on advancing our stories to monumental success.

To our Sisterhood Ambassadors of *The Fearless Storytellers Movement*:

Lenora Jones-Elliott
Aleida Salas
Sound Whisdom
Nikki Duncan Talley
Lakeisha Wilson
Angela Whitfield

Your stories are not just accounts of what *happened* to you but a collective, courageous tool to **energize, encourage, and empower** the heart of the soul who reads them.

Adrienne E. Bell
Fearless Storytellers Movement, Founder & CEO

DEDICATION

I dedicate this book to the women in my life who have and continue to inspire me.

My mother- Patricia – You were my first Shero! The one who taught me what strength looks like in human form. I love you and appreciate you more than you'll ever know!

My daughter- Jordyn- the main reason why I am still alive today. I've learned from you continuously since the day you were born. I'm so very proud of the woman you have become and continue to grow into.

My sister- Jatori- If resilience was a person- it would look exactly like you! You are Enough!!I value your presence in my world…. Never forget that! Thank you for all you do for me and the family!

My Aunties- Alberta, Margaret and Brenda Thank you for pouring into me when my cup ran dry! I appreciate each of you.

Last- to my cousins. Thank you for being more than cousins- many of you are like sisters to me and I am grateful!

To the sisters who stepped out on faith and shared their stories and experiences with us in this book – Thank You!

To Adrienne- Thank you for your patience with me and the sisters. You continued to support us even when life took over and we were side-tracked for one reason or another!

To the sisters who worked behind the scene to make this book a reality, Thank you!

Blessings to each of you- And know that I Love You Much!

Lenora

*"No matter how difficult it is, you must save yourself. Things external can never heal what's happening internally. It's your time to **HEAL FOR REAL!**"*

–Tamara

A LETTER TO MY SISTERS
Foreword by: *Tamara P. Fields, LCSW-S*

When I think about all the experiences I've had that should have ended my life, I often wonder about my sisters, who may have taken their own lives due to their emotional pain. The deep dark place that no one else understands. The place where you feel trapped with no exit in sight. The place that has completely paralyzed you. You often look in the mirror and wonder, *how did I even get here*? When did my life take a turn for the worse?

You were once happy, fun, and full of life. However, you have become so embarrassed about who you have become that you pushed everyone away. You're so afraid of being judged by others that you have suffered in silence for years. You wake up daily putting on your fake face to get through the day. When I think about my pain, I think about you, my sisters. I think about the experiences and struggles we share even though we've never met. We share the struggle to see the light at the end of the tunnel.

You have been going from bedroom to bedroom, alcohol to drugs, searching for peace. You attempt to find solace in one toxic relationship after another so that you are not alone. You were engaging in sex with men and women searching for love in all the wrong places, looking for relief from the pain. If only someone rescued you, this would all be over. I know those thoughts all too well. You were searching for something that would fill the void when the only thing required is **YOU**. It requires you to stop running, face your fears and deal with your pain. No matter how difficult it is, you must save yourself. Things external can never heal what's happening internally. **It's your time to heal FOR REAL.**

I know you feel so alone and broken, and you believe no one understands you. The truth is many women are struggling with you. You are not alone on this journey. Starting today, you will travel this road of healing with your sisters. Some you may know and many you've never met; however, you share the same story. Together you've decided to heal the pain of your past. Letting go of things and people who no longer serve you is the best decision of your life. We can not always control our experiences, but we can choose how we respond to them.

I know the journey ahead is scary but find comfort in the connection you are making with your emotions and women all around the globe healing with you. As you read this book and find yourself in these letters, remember **YOU ARE WORTHY!** Your life matters and you deserve everything your heart desires. I commend you for choosing yourself on this day. Thank you for being fearless in the pursuit of the new you. Enjoy what life has to offer on the other side of your pain.

With Love,
Your sister, Tamara

IN MY MEMORIES (INTRODUCTION)

In April 2021, my cousin Evelyn passed away. Months before she became ill, we had signed on to be one of my coaching clients. This was a little different because we grew up together. We lived 2 houses away from each other from the time I was 11 years old until I left to attend college.

When she passed away, I realized that there are so many things that we didn't get a chance to talk about. We made plans to do some things together, but because of life and the Corona Virus- those things never happened.

Whenever I see a post on social media in my memories about the plans we made, it pulls on my heart. I have all the would've, could've and should've feels deep in my spirit, so I decided to invite a few sisters to join me in writing a letter to our sisters. I really wanted to give an opportunity for sisters to share their thoughts and lessons they've learned on their journey!

This book is a compilation of stories and life lessons written by 7 beautiful sister-friends who agreed to allow us to have a peek into their worlds. They are sharing nuggets of wisdom they have experienced that could help someone else along the way.

I submitted 3 shorter stories instead of one long one. I wanted to do something a little different, as it will me share different parts of me with my sisters.

I truly believe that you will laugh, cry, shout Amen and even get super motivated by the messages shared between the covers of this book.

It takes a village – so as sisters of the village, we are taking this opportunity to pour out into you.

It is my prayer that something is said that will speak to your heard and your spirit.

Blessings to know!
Love Ya Much!
Lenora

RECLAIMING MY JOURNEY
By: Lenora Jones Elliott

Have you ever just wanted to tap out? You ever want to say You… Y'all….Everybody – You can have all of this because I've had Enough?

You're not angry, you're not upset…you're just tired!

Yep, I can relate.

I'm right there with you. I am tired and I want to throw in the towel.

I am tired of so many things. I am tired of the way things are and I'm frustrated because it seems like I am stuck. It is like I am spinning my wheels at getting anywhere.

Things in my world are just not where I want them to be. This is not where I thought I would be in life at my age. Twenty plus years ago I envisioned myself with a spouse, a house, my dream car, 2.5 children, the dog and a pool in the backyard. Unfortunately, that is not my reality right now. And no matter what I do at this very moment- I cannot force this vision into existence.

I finally got tired of being tired so I had to have a long hard talk with myself. I forced myself to face some serious areas in my life regarding my past and decisions I made along the way. I had to hold myself accountable for the things I did and the things I neglected to do. For the things I could not control- I extended myself grace. All the other things- I had to hold myself accountable. And that is when the work started.

I sat and created a list of all my hopes and dreams. The obtainable dreams and the ones that seemed beyond my reach. One by one, dream by dream, I added them to the list. My bucket list slowly morphed into prayers that turned into letters to God and my future self. I spelled out everything. It was like my whole soul was poured out onto the pages of my journal.

Next, I prioritized the list. As I started to move things around and highlight them with different colors, I realized that I had created a life map.

Once I completed the life map, I made a very startling discovery.

I'm not where I desire to be in life, but I have accomplishments that I can be proud of. I also realized that I pushed pass some trauma, generational curses and bouts of self-sabotage. I had to show myself some grace and acceptance for the things that I could not change along the way.

I learned that I had become so consumed with being sick and tired, that I neglected to live in the present. Because I was so critical of myself, I never fully celebrated my accomplishments.

If I could share an important life lesson with my sister right now, I would say – Be mindful of how you talk to yourself and how you treat yourself. Sometimes we are our worst critic. If the criticism is coming from another person, you can usually separate yourself from the source, but when the shots are being fired by your own brain- you may feel like there is no escape. Constant criticism in dangerous and it will drain the life out of you. This way of thinking can rob you of your future and that can hinder how you show up in spaces, if effect those who love you and those who have been assigned to your life.

At some point, you must say to yourself. Girl, you may not be where you want to be, BUT Thank God you're not where you use to be.

So, I would say to that sister. Get up, Dust yourself off and get back in the game. Don't tap out. The time has come for you to reclaim your life.

There is a saying," The journey of 1,000 miles begins with a single step."

Sister, the time has come for you to take that 1st step towards getting back on track.

I know it might not be an easy thing to do, but take that step in spite of the difficulty associated with it.

Even if you're afraid- take the step.

Your family, friends and members of your circle may not support what you're doing- step anyway.

People around you may discourage you – keep stepping!

Step until you get what you desire. Step until you get what you deserve. Step until you have what you dreamed of!

Remember, this ain't about them. Not everybody is going to applaud while you are on this journey, and that's ok. You have to be ok with that.

You applaud You! Become your biggest cheerleader instead of your biggest critic!

When you hear negative self-talk coming from your mouth, speak to it, call it under subjection and keep stepping forward.

You will get there. Someway…somehow….

Keep stepping, you will eventually Reclaim Your Journey!

"Telling my children that their father was gone was the hardest thing I ever had to do. Then it dawned on me, *I'm a single mother now.*"

– ***Angela***

THE SUN WILL COME UP TOMORROW

By: Angela Whitfield

Life is full of good and bad experiences. Some of us experience more bad than good at times and the bad will take you down if you let it. But there's always a day when the storm stops and the light shines through. As long as the sun comes up, you have a chance to make things better. This was a mantra I had to put to use instead of just saying it.

If I'm being honest, it was hard being my mother's daughter. She and I had a challenging relationship. My mother was controlling and always had an issue with my decisions. She held a lot of control over the things I did and the choices I made. I was in such bondage that I didn't make moves without her approval. My complicated relationship with my mother made for a life full of struggle and dependency that I didn't know existed.

I have a younger brother; he and I share the same parents. I also have an older brother; he and I share the same mother and have different fathers. When I was younger, my mother told me that my older brother was her favorite child. She loved his father immensely. She said she'd gotten pregnant with me on purpose to trap my father because he was financially stable at the time. Growing up, it was hard to get past that.

In 1993 my older brother joined the military and didn't look back. We didn't hear from him for 3 ½ years. Everything was okay until he left. When he left, my mother said she was done raising her kids, and she meant that. I was only 15-years-old when she left me and my younger brother to raise ourselves. We still lived with her, but her behavior changed drastically. She stopped coming home and stopped paying the bills. Sometimes we didn't have food in the house. Sometimes the lights were cut off. I had to get a job to help her out.

My mother was abusive mentally, emotionally, verbally, physically, and financially. She called me every vile name she could and would beat me often. My younger brother has a different story from mine and that of my older brother. He had his own struggles with her. My younger brother didn't have a curfew. He's two years younger than me and could do whatever he wanted to do. She didn't treat me like an adult. I had a curfew. My mother never respected me as an adult. She still saw me as a child once I became a woman. She didn't mistreat him the same way she mistreated me.

By the time my older brother came back, I had graduated high school. When he came back, my mother dropped everything for him. He was always in some kind of trouble, from jail stints to robbing our apartment. He even stole my paycheck a couple of times. She didn't care; she continued to let him stay. Unfortunately, he murdered someone during an armed robbery and went to prison. That is when my mother spiraled out of control. My older brother was her baby. She told me that she wished he and I could trade places. She could live without me but couldn't live without him. It was painful to hear her say that, and I believed her. I had no reason not to believe her. I know she meant what she said.

*****

My younger brother moved out when he was 17-years-old. By the time he left, I was an adult, and it was just me and my mom living together. It was 1997 and I was making $7.00/hr. I had to pay half of the bills. Not only that, I had to give her money to help her with her car payments. It wasn't fair. I was only 19-years-old.

I told her, "Ma, this doesn't work for me. I can't pay all your bills and I don't feel I should have to."

She told me she would think about what I said. One day, I came home to a note that essentially said she left and wasn't coming back. She had moved out and left me in the apartment one week before the rent was due. No conversation. Nothing.

Even though she left me in the apartment, she would say things like, "that apartment is still in my name, you better not mess anything up." So I started working three jobs just to make sure I could cover the rent. It was a constant struggle. I was working all the time and tired all the time. I was able to sleep for 1 to 2 hours per day. I couldn't keep up physically, and I could still barely afford the apartment and the bills.

Once, I gave her the money for the rent and asked her to hold it for me. I knew that if I kept it, I was going to do something else with it. I knew it was important to her to keep her credit right. When the rent was due, I went to get it back from her, and she told me she spent the money.

"It's gone," is what she told me. She had such an arrogant attitude about it. No explanation...nothing.

This was one of the first lessons I learned about my mom: *You can't trust your money with your mom.* By then, I'd been in the apartment for seven months. I was tired. I didn't know what to do, so I gave up and ended up getting evicted. After I'd gotten evicted, she bitched at me about not doing better.

I moved in with my younger brother and stayed for a year. We had a great time together. When the lease was up, my brother wanted to move to a more affluent part of town, which I couldn't afford, so I moved on by myself. Not moving with my brother was a bad decision. My brother and I were living two different lives, and I didn't think I could keep up. My younger brother flourished without my mom, but I didn't. He didn't need her, but I thought did.

My experience with my mother caused me extreme grief. It broke me as a person. She broke my spirit. My younger brother's experience with our mother motivated him to make sure he never needed her. Although we somewhat grew up in the same situation, we both took a different path. He had motivation that I didn't have. My brother was a hustler and worked hard.

I had to move where I could still get to work because I didn't have a car. That made it difficult to hold down a job. I lived in Chucksfield county in Richmond, Virginia. There was no public transportation where I lived, so I had to try to get a ride from someone every day. I was trying to maintain myself without depending on anyone else, but I was struggling.

My mother admitted to leaving me in a messed-up situation, so she offered to give me rides to work. I'd landed a good job working for a major telephone company. I think she was jealous and tried to sabotage me. She did things like pick me up late or not show up at all. I ended up losing that job.

I was born and raised in Chesterfield, Virgina, so I didn't have any other family in Richmond. My father was living in Mayland, strung out on drugs. I didn't see him for 12 years, from 11 to 23 years old. My mother was all I had. I *really* wanted to believe in her. Even though she failed me time after time, I kept relying on her. She kept telling me that I wasn't good enough and wasn't worth it. I made so many bad choices because of her. I didn't have anyone to guide me into making the right decisions. I lived a *very* hard life because of that.

* * * * *

It was 1999 and I was 21-years-old when I met a guy who was in the same situation as me. I was in a hotel room and he knocked on my door looking for someone else. He recognized me because we'd gone to school together. I didn't know him because he was older than me, but we had a lot of the same friends. The day he knocked on my door, we stood outside in the hallway, talking and laughing for two hours. We were together every day after that. He was struggling and having a difficult time with his family, too. He and I moved in together, and **it was just us.**

Of course, my mother didn't like him, and because she didn't like him, she made things hard for me. One day we didn't have any groceries and hadn't had anything to eat for two days. So I called my mother and asked her for help.

"I'll bring you a chicken. But he can't eat none," she said.

I told her, "then keep the chicken." Ahmad and I were in this **together.**

Ahmad was my best friend. He was the one that helped me see the control my mother had over me. I didn't realize it when it was happening because it was all I'd ever known. It wasn't abnormal to me. I thought everyone's parents were like that.

My mother refused to help me but expected me to call her every day. If I didn't, she'd come with the negativity. Ahmad and I lived on the streets for about seven months. I was 22-years-old. Sometimes we stayed in hotels until we couldn't afford it anymore. Other times, we slept on the streets. We both had to bounce a lot of checks just to have a roof over our head and food for the night. There were many days that left me feeling so low. I didn't even want to make it to the next day.

I was able to get a job working at the DMV in 2000. I called her and begged her to let me sleep on her floor until I got my first paycheck. I just wanted to get out of the hotel and off the streets. She let me stay until I got my first check. I got an apartment with my first check, and she complained, calling me selfish because I lived in her house for two weeks without buying her toiletries.

While staying with my mom for those two weeks, I had to leave Ahmad in the streets because she wouldn't let him stay. It was hard to leave him because I loved him. But it was the only way we were going to get out of that situation. Ahmad had gotten a job with Comcast in Maryland, so he moved. While he was working in Maryland, he sent money to me and came home on the weekends.

* * * * *

Ahmad and I were homeless together and got back on our feet together. When we got a place together, it wasn't in the best neighborhood. We were still living in a poverty-stricken neighborhood, but we were okay. We had a roof over our head, we had food, and we had lights. We still didn't have a car, but we were in a better place than we were previously.

In 2004, I was employed by the state and had gotten pregnant with my first child. Ahmad was still living and working in Maryland. I didn't want my child to go to daycare. I talked to Ahmad about what we were going to do. We agreed that Ahmad would quit his job, move back to Virginia and be a stay-at-home father. My daughter was born in November 2004.

In 2007, I had my second child, another girl. Now Ahmad and I had two kids, and I was still making the same amount of money I was when my first child was born. Ahmad and I had our problems. He was a stay-at-home parent, but he wasn't doing what he was supposed to do. He didn't wash dishes or keep up with any of the household chores. Sometimes I'd come home, and he hadn't cooked anything, or I'd come home to all his friends being at our house. Life was rough when our second child arrived, but I worked through it.

We never had a plan to get married. We wanted to get married, but it wasn't a priority because we were together so much. Not only that, a wedding costs money, which we didn't have a lot of. One day I was at work when I called Ahmad.

"We should just go get married," I said.

"Okay," he quickly responded.

I left work and we went to the courthouse to get a marriage license. Ahmad and I married on Wednesday, January 30, 2008, at 8 pm. No one else was there. Just Ahmad and me. We didn't call anybody. We had our third child in 2009, a boy.

*****

I was well in my 30's before I experienced any loss. I still had my parents and grandparents. In 2011, my maternal grandmother passed. That was extremely hard for me. I'd never seen someone I loved so much in a casket. **I was devastated.** Every year after that, I lost another family member. My grandfather passed away in 2012. In 2013, I lost an uncle, my father in 2014, and in 2015, I lost my paternal grandmother. In 2016, I lost another uncle. In 2017, I lost a close friend. But the loss I experienced in 2018 nearly took me out.

I didn't think we were in a bad place, but I noticed Ahmad had been acting weird all week. He was agitated the entire week. Ahmad and I went to his father's house for the 4th of July. My brother-in-law, Ahmad, and I were having a conversation about the benefits at my job. I don't remember if I corrected him in that conversation or gave him some misinformation, but the following day he woke up with an attitude. Ahmad having an attitude wasn't uncommon. There was always somebody he didn't like. Anyway, Ahmad told me he was upset with Fakier, his brother.

"Why?" I asked him.

He said Fakier looked at him strangely. I thought, *what?*

"I didn't see him look at you strangely," I clarified. Ahmad became angry that I hadn't noticed his brother looking at him oddly. Ahmad started going off on me the entire day.

"You don't ever notice anything…" "You don't have my back…" "I don't know how you didn't see him looking at me like that…" He kept going on and on.

"Ahmad, you need to calm down. If you have that much of an issue, Fakier is the one you need to talk to, not me. You're not going to keep arguing with me all day about how another grown-ass man looked at you." I had to put things in perspective so he could calm down.

We argued every day until July 8, 2018. I woke up that morning, and Ahmad was already up, which was odd. He was still talking about his brother and this supposed look he gave him.

"Look, I'm not gon' do this with you, not one more day. If you have a problem with Fakier, I suggest you man up and go talk to him."

"Fine, I'll do that," he responded.

He walked out of the house. It was hot that day, and Fakier didn't live anywhere near us, so I didn't know where he was going. I began cooking breakfast for the kids. I wanted a Pepsi and didn't have any, so I drove to the store to grab a Pepsi. As soon as I got in the car, Ahmad called me, asking me to pick him up.

"Sure," I told him. "Where you at?"

He said, "I'm up the street."

I was close to the store and stopped when I saw him. He got in the car and didn't say anything to me. He was staring out the window. I parked the car at the store and asked him if he was going inside with me. He didn't respond. He just got out of the car and walked towards the store with me. He sat on the bench outside the store instead of going inside with me. He was acting odd.

I'll be honest; I'm a bit of a bitch. I'd been dealing with his attitude enough, and I wasn't going to cater to it. I didn't say anything to him. I got what I needed from the store, and when I walked out of the store, he looked at me but didn't get up from the bench. I looked back at him.

Confused, I asked, "Are you coming?"

He didn't say anything. He got up and walked behind me to the car. As we were leaving the store, we made a left, driving towards our apartment.

"Where are you going?" He asked me.

"Home."

"No, take me to Ashley's house." Ashley is his sister.

"I'm in the middle of cooking. Just take the car," I told him.

I bought Ahmad a gun as a gift and he always carried it. He patted his waist where he kept the gun and told me, "No, you're gonna take me there right now!"

"You're going to your sister's house with a gun? It's that serious?"

He said, "Take me over there or you'll never see me again."

I didn't understand what was going on. He carried on about how I don't ever understand him.

"Just take me to my sister's house!" He demanded. At this point, I was scared. I had never seen him act like that. He'd never spoken to me like that. He didn't point the gun at me, but I felt threatened.

I was worried about him and worried for his sister. Once we got to her neighborhood, I pulled over on a side street because I didn't know exactly where she lived. I wasn't willing to take him any further. My plan was to let him out of the car, and while he was walking to her house, I was going to call and warn her. I felt like she needed a heads up.

Once he got out of the car, he stood there with the door open, looking at me.

"I always knew it was gonna be you."

Still, in a state of confusion, I said, "you always knew it was gonna be me to what?"

He said, "Get out the car!"

"No, I'm good."

Next thing I know, he reached in the car and punched me on the side of my face.

"Bitch, I said get out the car!"

He'd never called me out of my name and definitely had never hit me before. I still didn't know what was going on but I knew this was completely out of character for him.

He tried to take the keys out of the ignition, but couldn't because my foot was on the brake, and the car was still in drive. He took my cell phone and wallet.

He said it again. "I said get out of the car!" This time he was pointing the gun at me. He reached in the car and punched me on the side of my face again. I realized either I had to get out of the car or he was going to beat the shit out of me. So I took my seatbelt off and got out of the car. He walked around the vehicle to the driver's side, where I was standing, and aimed the gun at me. I put my hands up.

"Ahmad, what the fuck is wrong with you?"

He looked at me and said, "you gon' die today."

Oh, shit. He was serious. I looked around, surveilling my surroundings. No one was around. I knew running wasn't an option. I was standing in the middle of the street with the person I love telling me he was about to kill me. I kept walking backwards as he kept inching towards me. An old Geo Metro drove by with two ladies inside. They slowed down, but didn't stop completely. So I pulled at their car door. It was unlocked, so I jumped in and said, "he has a gun."

The driver sped off, tires screeching, and took me around the corner.

"You're bleeding. You need medical help," she said to me.

My face was split open from him hitting me. I had no idea I was even bleeding. I took my shirt, wiped my face, and saw all the blood. She drove me to the police station. I didn't have anybody's phone number because Ahmad had my phone. I didn't know anyone's number by heart except for my brother. So I called him, and he answered.

"Ahmad punched me in my face. I'm at the police station. I need you to go get my kids."

One of my kids was already with my brother.

"I'm on the other side of town, but I'm on my way," He assured me.

As I was sitting at the police station, I thought about Ashley. I couldn't call her because I didn't know her number and didn't have my phone. I told the police that they needed to find her house because that's where Ahmad was headed. One of the police officers walked in the station and said to another officer, "they found him DOA."

He wasn't speaking to me, and as I reflect, I didn't think they were talking about Ahmad. They could've been talking about anyone.

One of the officers informed me that another officer would be taking my statement. The officer never came. I was told that he was caught up on another case. They asked me if there was anyone I could call that would be able to give me a ride home. I called my brother again. He finally arrived to pick me up a few minutes later. Before I left, I asked the officer, "can I go get my car?"

He said, "I mean, you can, but it's an active crime scene. They're still looking for your husband. So I don't know if you want to."

I had my brother with me, so I felt safe to do so. He took me to where I left my car, but it wasn't there. It was parked in the middle of the street with all the windows rolled down. I looked inside to see if Ahmad had left the keys inside the car. They weren't there, and neither was my phone or my wallet. I sat inside my car and used my brother's phone to call a tow truck. My brother was walking around the area to ensure Ahmad wasn't lurking somewhere or about to walk up on us. He walked back to me.

"Hey Ang, there's a lot of police down the street. There's crime scene tape down there."

We wanted to be nosey, so we walked down the street to see what was going on. The closer we got, I recognized the police officer that was supposed to come back to the station, take my statement, and drive me home.

"Did somebody call you?" The officer asked me.

"Call me for what? No, nobody called me. I just walked down here from my car." I didn't know what he was talking about.

"Stay right here. I'm going to get somebody to come talk to you." He turned around and walked away from me. I could see a body lying in the grass. **It was Ahmad.**

My first thought was, *the police shot him.* The detective walked up to me and told me that Ahmad had killed himself. **I hit the ground.** Ahmad was my very best friend. A true partner. We literally grew up together. That day I became a 40-year-old widow. I'd never felt so much numbness come over me at one time. I felt nothing. *Nothing at all.*

On July 8, 2018, my husband killed himself. It was an attempted murder/suicide. He tried to take me with him. He didn't leave a note or an explanation. To this day, I still don't truly know what made him so angry that he'd commit suicide. I sat outside with him until the coroner picked him up. I couldn't leave him out there by himself. After everything that happened that day, I still loved him so much. I knew his behavior that day wasn't a representation of the person I knew. That wasn't the man that loved me for 20 years.

Telling my children that their father was gone was the hardest thing I ever had to do. Then it dawned on me, *I'm a single mother now.* Just that fast, my whole life changed. When I walked inside my brother's house, my children knew something was wrong because they saw my face all torn up. Immediately they were concerned.

"What happened to your face?" One of my babies asked.

"Your father did it."

"What happened?" They kept probing. No one could believe he'd hit me because everyone witnessed how much Ahmad loved me.

"Your dad didn't make it," They screamed. I'd never heard anyone scream like that in my life. My heart broke in pieces all over again. I'd just lost my father as an adult so I knew how bad they were hurting as children. I didn't know how to console them.

"How'd he die?" They asked me. And I had to tell them the truth. I don't lie to my kids, so I told them everything that happened. Two of my kids came home with me that night; my middle daughter didn't. She didn't come home for *days*. She stayed at my brother's house. I had to *make* her come home. Ahmad committed suicide one month before her 11th birthday.

Ahmad taught them **everything.** He was a stay-at-home father, so he was there for their first steps. He taught them how to walk, talk, read and write. I was sacrificing for my family. I worked and paid the bills. I became a single parent to three kids that I didn't really *know.* My oldest daughter was 13, my middle daughter was 10, and my son was 8 when their father passed away.

This was the moment I had to take my own advice. I'd always say, *"the sun will come up tomorrow, and if it doesn't, you don't have anything to worry about."* I had to ask myself, *did I really believe that? Or was it just something that sounded good?* I decided I really believed it. I had no choice but to believe it.

He took his life, not mine. I had a moment of feeling grateful. Grateful that he didn't pull the trigger when the gun was aimed at me. Grateful that that car passed by when it did. I was grateful because I realized that when the detective told me he was dead, I knew he would really kill me. He wasn't playing around. That was a hard pill to swallow.

I had never planned a funeral though I had attended so many before. The following day my in-laws called me and told me they were at the Waffle House up the street. They wanted me to bring the kids so they could talk to us. When we arrived, my in-laws were very concerned about my face. They wanted me to get medical attention, but I hadn't yet been to a doctor. They insisted on keeping the kids while I went to get my face checked out.

"Where is Ahmad?" My father-in-law asked me.

"I don't know. I don't know where he is," I replied. I'll be honest; I was drunk. I avoided the pain by staying drunk. It was the only way I could cope day to day. Later that day, I called around and found out that Ahmad's body was at the city morgue. My father-in-law paid for Ahmad's funeral. I only had to show up and sign documents. I don't know why but I thought that funeral homes had people that wrote obituaries. *No.* I had to write his obituary. I was not too fond of the idea of a person being buried, so I chose cremation. The day before the memorial service, the funeral home called me to tell me that I needed to come to the funeral home and sign a document so he could be transported to the crematorium. I asked them if I had to see Ahmad's body. They told me I didn't. I asked the kids if they wanted to see their father. They said no. I asked my father-in-law to go with me. He didn't want to. I called my brother-in-law, Ahmad's younger brother, to go with me. He agreed to go.

When we arrived, they walked us upstairs to a white door with frosted glass in the middle. The funeral home told us we were free to walk inside. When I opened the door, there was my husband, laying on a flag with a towel wrapped around his head. I hit the floor again. Now it was real. He was gone. I screamed so loud. It was such a sunny day, but the moment I started screaming, I heard thunder outside. The sky opened up, pouring down rain. By the time I walked out of the funeral home, the rain had stopped. It was sunny again. Everything in my spirit told me that the shift in weather was Ahmad. I knew he was sorry for what he did.

I was late to the funeral because my son had stopped sleeping. He would sit up all night. The morning of the funeral, he passed out, and I couldn't wake him up. I drove myself to the funeral. When I reached the funeral home, there were hundreds of people lining the funeral home walls outside. He would've never believed that many people would show up to his funeral. He swore I was the only person that loved him, but that turnout showed otherwise.

Ahmad was in the military at one point. I was presented with the flag. When the funeral was over, they handed me Ahmad's urn wrapped in a towel inside of a box. It was still hot from the cremation the day before. I held that hot ass urn on my chest. I knew that was going to be the last time I would feel any kind of heat from him. Then I went home. I didn't want to attend any repasses.

I brought him home and stayed there for a month, *drunk*. I couldn't sleep because I hadn't slept by myself in over 20 years. I had a friend that would come over every night for a year and sleep in the bed with me. About four months after my husband died, I realized if I didn't stop drinking, this would be my new life. And that's not what I wanted. So I stopped. I accepted that he took his life, not mine. I couldn't stop living just because he chose to.

*****

I couldn't fall because I'm a mother. I had to stand strong so that my children would have someone to lean on. I got back up and found my life again. Things were going well until I received a phone call while I was at work from my aunt.

"I found your mom unresponsive," She told me.

"Call 911," I told her. But she told me they were already there.

"Did you try to wake her up? What's wrong with her?" I fired questions at her.

"I don't know. I think you should come."

I called my brother, who was three hours away in Virginia Beach.

"Mommy is sick," I told him. I was freaking out. I mean, it's my momma. Of course, I felt the panic inside. I jumped in my car and headed towards my mother's house in the country. The drive was about an hour. The whole way there, my aunt kept calling me, saying to hurry up because people were there waiting for me. I was irritated. *What people was she talking about?*

When I was about 25 minutes away, I called my aunt and asked her what hospital my mom was at.

"Don't go to the hospital. Come to the house."

"Joann, please, don't let me walk in, and my momma is dead. Tell me now," I told her.

"Baby, I'm sorry. She's gone."

I was speeding and got pulled over. When the police officer got to my car window, I told him that I needed to go because my mother had passed away. He said okay.

When I got there, my mom was in a bag. I couldn't look at her face. I sat on the floor and held her hand. It still felt like her. She hadn't gone cold yet. I had to plan a funeral...*again*.

She called me so many times the week she died and asked me to visit her, but I refused. My mother passed away in her sleep, 10 months after my husband died.

At that point, my mother and I had mended our relationship. She was still her, but she apologized for the things she did to me. She was a great grandmother to my children, and I felt like I was a horrible daughter. My mother moved to the country, and I refused to go see her. I was hurt that she brought me to Virginia and just left me when she moved. So I harbored that resentment. She always called me and asked me to come out to her place. But I wouldn't. When she passed, that was something that I thought about constantly.

The little girl in me is still hurting. When I was young, I didn't have an understanding of life or people. I don't think my mom had disdain for me. I think she was scorned because she didn't do the things she wanted to do in life. I don't hold anything against my mother. I love her. We all have decisions to make and sometimes those decisions are poor choices. A lot of her choices weren't for my benefit. The situation I was in with my mother was extremely unfortunate. Her choices were painful and affected me deeply. If I could, I would go back and tell my younger self, *you're going to be okay.*

When I think about everything I've endured over the years, I can't help but cry. The grief didn't crush me and I'm so grateful for that. Even with all that I've lost, I know I have to keep living. The grief is heavy, and I carry it with me every day. I'm still dealing with all of it. I can't say I'm completely healed, but I still smile, and I'm proud of myself. I am proud of you, too. The only thing we can do moving forward is keep taking steps forward because the sun will come up tomorrow.

"Do not be afraid to walk away and protect your peace at all costs."

–*Aleida*

A BAG OF BROKEN PIECES

By: Aleida Salas

I hope that once you all have read this journey that your view of me does not scream whore, loose, etc. but more so looked upon as courageous and victorious. Closure is very necessary to move forward in life. Without this, you can never fully flourish into your destiny or have healthy relationships instead most of them would be fractured or seen through jagged lenses. My hope is that all my sisters who read my story walk away with a whole different mindset and a newfound confidence to walk away from "situation ships" that are not going to fulfill you. I hope you will embrace loving yourselves 100 percent.

Names have been changed or altered.

When I met him, I was 19 years old and had just come home for summer break from college. I headed across the street to a family friend's house that we went to school with. House was full and there were card games going on and everyone just chilling and having a good time. As soon as I walked in the door, my friend Brad welcomed me, and it was clear he was a little toasted but none the less I was happy to see him. As I walked in, I greeted everyone then heard Brad say, "here is my brother Stephen…. Stephen meet Aleida". before I knew it, I was like "damn he is fine", to myself.

Our eyes locked and the next thing I knew it was like the whole room stopped and we were the only ones in there. He immediately swept me off my feet. Him calling me turned into visits on the weekends until we were seeing each other almost every day when he got off work. Our meeting spot was at the family friends house across the street. We were good for a while and love had its way with him.

One day he and I rode out to where he lives and when we got there, he stopped by the neighborhood corner store so he could get a pack of cigarettes. As I waited for him in the car, I noticed a couple of guys that I knew. They walked up and asked me how I was doing. After chit chatting for a moment Stephen walked out and greeted the guys. I am from a small area where everyone lived next door to each other. They guys knew Stephen's brothers, so it was all love.

A couple of days passed, and I get a call from one of the sisters across the street. She was threatening me, talking about she was going to let Stephen's girlfriend know about me. Now of course I didn't know he had a girlfriend at the beginning, but I was able to paint the picture that it was complicated, and they were basically not together. He said he was going to leave her blah, blah, blah and like a dummy I believed him. In about a week or so, I noticed he wasn't coming to see me as much anymore. It became less, and less that I was talking to him on the phone.

One night he showed up at my house unexpectedly to tell me he couldn't see me anymore and he was in tears as was I. I always felt like he had fallen in love with me not meaning to, because of the emotion he showed when he ended it with me. (I will not call it a breakup because that would be a lie). He was more concerned about protecting my feelings, knowing he had to walk away from me. That was the end. At least at that moment. This was the summer of 1994/1995 (do not quote me on the years because I do not remember)....

My next mistake goes by the name of Everett. He was also in my freshman/sophomore year in college. When we met it started off as a friendship. Every time we saw each other he was always talking smack. We would talk it back and forth with each other until we developed an attraction for one another. Next thing you know, we had an intimate encounter. Afterwards, things became strained and then the playfulness turned into insults.

My best friend at the time did not appreciate the fact that he was going around saying that he was shooting blanks when we both know that was a lie. Everett was a self-absorbed narcissist who glorified himself on being loud and trying to embarrass others for his personal satisfaction. Needless to say, we became enemies and after the school semester/year he ended up leaving college and we did not have any more communication with one another for years....

Fall semester of my sophomore year was when I met another loud-mouthed immature male who goes by the name of Khalil. Khalil was from DC. Still to this day, I cannot put my finger on what was so appealing about him that made me attracted to him other than his sense of humor. And well, ladies, you already know what else. Anyway, when I first met him, it was while hanging out around the boy's dorm. I was around twenty at the time (I do not know the year so please forgive me). Me and my home girl at the time were sitting on the step outside and he was coming down the steps to pass by me. He sparked up a conversation with me and as the days went on, we started to hang out with each other. We hung out a lot until gradually a kiss turned into a hug and then turned into an encounter behind one of the buildings on campus. Afterwards, things became different between us until we no longer spoke anymore. I would see him and go to speak to him, and he would act like he did not know me anymore. This closed this chapter of brokenness. I then left him on read…. forever….

Kristoff Garrett walked into my life at the beginning of my junior year like a breath of fresh air. He was different, not like the usual. He had a swag that was unusual and magnetic. His best friend was the same. They both were like chocolate and vanilla with a sense of humor that was "off the chain".

Because I had always been considered a "black sheep" or a "loner" myself, I was able to understand him, and he could always confide in me about anything without reserve or the thought of me looking at him differently. This was a special friendship that turned "situationship" because he was so transparent with me and I with him. Unfortunately, he ended up involved in a fight with the DC/Maryland guys and the baseball team, which landed him suspended for the remainder of the semester.

A couple of days before leaving we shared a kiss and our feelings. When I saw him off that day, I cried but knew that we would see each other again. So, fast forward to year 2000 (again please do not quote me on the year), I had graduated college and began my new journey in life. I moved with my best friend to the tidewater area of Virginia. Kristoff was on my mind, and we had begun to communicate off and on prior to me getting there. He is originally from Newport News, Virginia but lived in Hampton, Virginia.

When I got there, we picked up right where we left off, only this time the feelings were much stronger and eventually grew into an actual relationship. As time went on, his priorities began to change; or should I say, he started to show his true colors. His priorities became more about his "boys", his liquor and his weed instead of finding a job, keeping a job and growing together until I broke it off with him. For a while were doing our own thing until I got a phone call that he got "locked up" (arrested) for being a follower. He and his friends robbed someone's house and when they got caught, he was left with the bag. After visiting him in jail he claimed he was going to get his "ish" together. Of course things went from bad to worse.

The inconsistencies got worse, the drinking increased and so did the smoking. I was working two jobs at the time and when I would leave, he would be in the bed like a kid eating cereal. When I would return home he was still in the same position. The epiphany came when we were trying to have an intimate moment and he was so inebriated he passed out.

That was when I knew he had to go. He was in a stooper, so I pushed him off me on to the floor and he hit the wall. He woke up the next morning wondering how he got down there and that is when I told him to get out. I loved him and it hurt but he had to go.

Four years later, he tried to reach out to me again from Idaho and then that was last I heard of him completely. Moral of this story is you cannot make somebody act right unless they want to or are ready to do so. Also, you cannot make somebody love you when they do not even love themselves. It will always be an endless cycle….

While in between finding a place to stay and staying with a good friend, I was working at a call center. I met Daniel. We were in the same training class and became close after we got to the floor. A lot of us from work use to hang out together a lot after work at my one-bedroom apartment. From there we forged a bond. It was strictly just a close friendship at the time, an didn't want to ruin the friendship. He was living with his baby's mother, and they were off and on.

One day we were hanging out and I was in my room not able to hold back the feelings any longer. He came upstairs and sat on the bed and I braced myself and told him. He then began to say he felt the same which led to what should not have happened (never ever sleep with your best friend).

It happened once, or twice and it altered the friendship. So, one day after work, Daniel introduced me to a good friend of his by the name of Keith. Supposedly, Daniel's whole angle was to see me happy because he could not be with me like he wanted to, due to the fact that he was still with his baby's mother.

Because I thought this gesture came from a genuine place of him having my best interest at heart, I could do nothing but respect him for wanting to see me happy, even if it would mean that I would not be with him. When I agreed to go out with Keith, I did not know that this would change my life drastically and do some irreversible damage.

This relationship or saga was one that was the most difficult for me to tell, especially with all the emotional damage that it did to me. The one date with Keith turned into a spark, and I fell in love with him effortlessly. The love I had for him and him for me was true, passionate, and beautiful. He use to cook for me because he worked as a chef. He ran my bath when I got off work. He would feed me dinner and then we would make endless love. It was bliss…. until Daniel's attitude started to change towards me.

Us hanging out almost began to be nonexistent and he became jealous because Keith was always with me. One night Daniel and Keith almost got into an argument, but I intervened. It was clear that Daniel felt "some kind of way" about the relationship. Life went on and love was going strong with Keith and I. I could not be happier.

My home girl at the time leaked to me that Keith was going to propose to me and had already bought the ring, but I had to act like I did not know. She told me he was going to surprise the next day with it. I was so ecstatic it was hard for me to contain myself. So, to rewind a bit, this was where things went left.

We had just finished being intimate and I was laying in the bed, and he went to go use the bathroom and when he did, he noticed that there was an issue down below. Of course, I knew it was not me, but we felt it was nothing to be alarmed about, so I left to go home because it was time for my women's annual and he said he was just going to go to the ER, and have it checked out, but he felt like it was really nothing to worry about. We both trusted each other and were with each other most of the time so there was no cheating involved.

After my pap and the standard other tests you get came back, the doctor comes back and tells me that I have gonorrhea. At first, I looked at at this doctor like she had three heads. I have always been an exceptionally clean woman and I didn't lay down with everybody, so I knew this had to be a mistake. And of course, I had no doubt where he was concerned. All the thoughts of a wedding, a family, and being happy just went right down the drain. So, I broke down crying all the way home and I felt like my whole world was completely shattered at that very moment.

When I got home, I got myself together as best as I could because this was the day that Keith was supposed to propose to me, and I knew that this was going to be the end of us once I told him. When I got there, there were rose petals on the floor when I walked in going to the bed, the smell of a wonderful meal being prepared, and music playing. I believe it was Jodeci playing, my favorite. When I embrace him, he hugged and kissed me, but his face was of stone, emotionless.

I also noticed that he had not called me the whole day which was strange but considering what I had just found out I already knew what was happening. I broke down again when I saw his face and he asked me what was wrong in a very monotone way. That is when I told him what the doctor said and then the evening was more or less ruined. Then when I saw the ring box sitting on the table by the candles and the wonderful meal, he prepared I was no more good.

He hugged me and watched over me the whole night. He never told me what his results were from when he went to the ER, but I figured that is why he had his meds. The next day I woke up in the same condition because I knew I was going to lose him and all I could keep telling him over and over is that I did not cheat and that I loved him. He kissed me of my forehead that morning with the same cold look on his face and said that he would talk to me later but did not say I love you. I got on the bus and cried all the way home and when I waked through the door, I could tell the message light was blinking on my answering machine. It was then that I knew what I was going to hear and when I pushed play messages his was the first one saying he was breaking up with me. He could not bring himself to tell me to my face.

After hearing that, I was completely done, and I cried uncontrollably the whole day. For days I cried nonstop. I was so hurt. That is when I had to sit and think who or how I could have gotten this disease when I had only been with him, and he was not cheating. Once the smoke cleared, it then came to me after I went back some months......(lesson: in case some of y'all don't know, a woman can have gonorrhea for months and not know she has symptoms but if it gets passed to a man, he will know instantly or within a few days he will start to show symptoms). When I sat and thought about it, it all became clear. This is when the anger came. It was that fuckin' Daniel who gave it to me because he was the last person I was intimate with and men know when they have it, which means he gave it to me knowing he had it.

I had been carrying It around for months unaware. When I got with Keith, I passed it along to him unknowingly. I became even more devastated. On top of all if that, I lost my job, and my apartment. I had 10 days to vacate and did not know where I was going to live.

I feel into a deep depression at this point. I felt like I had lost everything, and I tried to commit the unthinkable. Oh, but God though. I looked in the mirror while I was sitting in my muck and mire and said, "Aleida what are you doing?" God knocked that knife right out of my hand and got me together quick.

As time went on, I became bitter and hated all men and that lasted for a few years. I was so jagged and jaded that I did not even like myself. The toxic energy I was giving off was awful and I ended up alienating everyone. All the people closest to me, who loved could not put up with me anymore.

Ok so a year passed, and I began working at a cell phone store in the mall during the day and had a second job in the evenings. Even though I still was not completely healed, I was still holding onto hope that he would come back to me one day. A lot of what I was holding on to was guilt and not so much love, but I was very broken still and damaged.

One day I walked into work, and beside the cell phone place was a great little restaurant that sold Chinese food and subs. As I was walking by, I happened to turn my head and there he was back there doing what he loved to do best and that was cooking. I thought I was going to pass out and that God had answered my prayers.

He looked up and we locked eyes. He then signaled me to come in and we had a conversation which I was even shocked that he wanted to say anything to me. I was so elated and happy. All of those old feelings from when we were together stirred up and before I knew it, we were working on getting back together. He said that he never fell out of love with me and that he knew I didn't cheat or intentionally set out to hurt him.

After a month or two we seemed to be on our way. One night he invited me to his place and when I arrived, there was a chic there and she was posted up chilling and smoking. She glanced at me and then back at the tv, I thought nothing of it because I know he does not like to smoke alone, and she was his neighbor. Nothing seemed off and we were just talking still at the time and not back together officially, so I left it alone. I sat there and hung out for a while and then left and went home.

The next time I went over there we became intimate for the first time after reconnecting, and I was so elated but afterwards something felt off. We were so intense with each other that I felt like he was trying to either get me pregnant or he just missed me that much. We continued communicating, but he was somewhat nonchalant with me. The very last time I saw him again was when he invited me over but when I get there and knocked on the door, I heard a female's voice laughing along with him.

It was cold outside and late at night and he lived 30-40 minutes away from me. I saw him peek outside and he acted as if he didn't know I was outside and told her oh it's just her and they both laughed. So, I left with my tail tucked between my legs and feeling hurt and stupid.

A couple of weeks later I was standing at the bus stop and not feeling very well. As a matter of fact, I hadn't been feeling well for the last week in a half. I knew I had been going through a lot, feeling emotionally drained, and still broken, but this particular day I felt really off. The bus was pulling up and as It was coming closer, I started seeing black spots and just when I was about to faint the bus opened its doors just in time.

Later that evening, I had one of my friends take me to the ER because I just wasn't feeling right. I sat there and waited on the results from a pregnancy test, which I just knew that I was not pregnant. After waiting for about an hour, the doctor comes back to me with "Miss Salas your 2 weeks pregnant and you have Trich". I was devasted, angry, and broken down even further, I felt naive and stupid.

I was too scared to call Keith and tell him this news when I got home because I didn't know what his reaction would be. When I got up enough nerve to call him, he had the chick to answer the phone laughing and she hands him the phone. When I told him I was pregnant and had "trich" he pauses for a minute and then said, "Now you know how it feels to be on the receiving end and I don't know how you could be pregnant with a polluted womb". He then hung up on me.

Now I was faced with what decision I was going to make. I had no money, was struggling, was only making $5.15 pressing pants in the cleaners, was almost $1,000 in the whole in my rent and there I was pregnant and intentionally given an STD out of revenge. Needless to say, I did what I had to do. I was not proud of what I did but I was already in a bad place in my life at that time. I definitely didn't need to bring another person into the world that would be depending on me and I not be able to provide for them. I didn't want to be another statistic. I struggled with forgiving myself for a while……

When broken pieces continue to pile on top one another, it becomes harder to see through lenses that are not defective because when you have been hurt so much and so deeply, defective lenses become normal to you along with a toxic mindset and jagged view. Because I didn't pass the assignment the first time, God gave it to me again through a guy named James. He was a cook at Cheddar's restaurant, and I met him one day while out getting lunch. We struck up a conversation and started seeing each other at once. After seeing each for two weeks, I found myself once again, pregnant and with another STD. At this point I had no one else to blame but myself. When I told him he asked me "how do I know it's his and that he wasn't doing shit and hung up. I never heard from him again and I once again, I did what I had to do. So now my self-worth was definitely questionable at this point. More broken pieces……

Now Carl was another pivotal moment in my life that really made me take back control of my standards, values, and self-worth. I gravitated towards him because he had an edge about him that I loved. He was outspoken in a sexy take charge kind of way. He was not necessarily a street dude, but I was so fragile at the time I felt protected by him in a strange sort of way.

Three of my closest friends could not stand him. They were worried about me being with him and for my safety. Carl was verbally abusive and could cut you with his tone and his words. I tried to show him that I was here for him and that whatever obstacles we faced, we could face them together. He used to always fight against me and really didn't treat me like his woman. I was so busy pouring into him, that I had nothing left to give myself. He was draining me. The more I tried, the more he became volatile towards me and shut me out.

I had a part time job at the time, and he did not work. He had every excuse as to why he couldn't work. Things were getting tight financially, so he ended up selling street pharmaceuticals at night and would come back in the morning. I noticed that he would come back with next to nothing after being out all night.

Vice would sit out and watch because the area I lived in at the time was "Crack Central", so it was no way he was going to tell me that it was a slow night. As time went on, gradually stuff started disappearing out of my place after I let him bring a girl in. He said was his friend who was homeless and needed someplace to stay, so I let her stay on the couch.

I went to work one day and when I returned home, my place was in shambles and my friends who occupied the other room was packing their things. When I asked what happened, they said Vice came in and raided the place. They arrested Carl after they saw him coming back and forth that day. They found $1,000 in cash, a pound of weed and some crack rock under my mattress.

By the grace of God, the landlord said that I could still stay there since I had nothing to do with it, nor was I there when it went down. So here I was trying to be the supportive girlfriend. I called his boys to see if they could scratch up some bail money and of course they claimed to not have it. When I called down to booking and asked to speak with him, he blamed me for having him sitting up in there. He said if I loved him, I would find the money to get him out. I told him that I was trying, and he straight hung up on me.

Since he had never been arrested before, he was being let out on his own recognizance. After the hearing was over and he was processed out, he began to call me all types of bitches and that I did not give a fuck about him because I didn't have the money to get him out. He did this in front of the courthouse, in front of everyone. Because he couldn't stay with me anymore, he was staying at a friend's house.

The time away from him allowed me to think about what I was allowing him to do to me and that I am worth way more than this treatment. I packed up what little shit he had and sat it by the door with a note attached saying "I want you and you shit gone by the time I get back". Sure enough, he met me at the bus and as I was getting off. He gave me back the keys and that chapter was closed….

This takes me to the next idiot who was also a mistake and a big lesson. Do not ever think friends with benefits is a prerequisite or foundation towards a relationship. When I boarded the bus on my way to work, I could feel him constantly staring at me and I stared back. He was very smooth with his approach. I couldn't knock him because it was respectful, but you could tell he was definitely on a mission. He could visibly see that I was a BBW yet that did not stop him. We exchanged a few words an then we exchanged numbers.

His name was Devaughn 22 years old which was a mistake right there in itself. I was twenty-eight at the time. As we started seeing each other the more I saw his cocky, arrogant side start to rear his ugly head. You see, he thought his 12-inch manhood made him a man and that BBW's are nothing but dead fish in the bedroom. Of course, I proved him wrong. Feelings on both sides began to grow. But what destroyed the friendship was the fact that he could not bring himself to admit that he had strong feelings and for a BBW. He claimed that all the women he dealt with were model type chic's. So, he began to keep me hidden or a secret. I am nobody's "creep piece" neither was I the fat girl you come and see at night. Trust, I had him walking to my house to get this, so it looks to me like he was the one sprung but claimed he did not feel for me in that way.

One night he bought his best friend over to meet me. The best friend told him how stupid he was and that he was making a big mistake. I had to keep telling this" n***a" that he was not the only one that could pull his share of chics. I told him best believe this BBW pulls them on a daily so stop playing with me. His best friend then tried to hit on me, but of course I declined because I am not like that. When I told him, he became upset. I said to him I do not know why you are upset because you claim you did not want me, so why would this make you upset.

He could not answer. He then went further to insult me by saying I hope you do not think a guy is going to take you out to dinner and not try to hit it. I said so you think all fat girls are good for is sex? He then laughed so I told him if we are just platonic, then what is your issue. I told him I could drop 150 pounds by getting rid of his ass, I threw him out and slammed the door. That was the end of that. He tried to call one or two more times for a late-night creep, and I declined. I told him never to call my number again. The lesson here is to know you're more than enough so embrace and love all parts of you.

Let us move forward to 2009-2010. Stephen enters back into the picture like 15 years later. Somewhere around 2009 we reconnected through social media after all these years. Remember y'all, I was 19 years old when we first got together. I was young, so he was meeting Aleida the woman. I believe I was 29-30 years old by this time. I had lived some life and had some additional scars.

He was going through an awfully hard time and had recently broken up with his girlfriend (so that was the shit he kicked to me). Anyway, we started talking again and all those emotions came flooding back. It was like I was in love all over again. We stayed up sometimes talking on the phone til the wee hours of the morning, then I would get up and get ready for work. He said that he was starting all over again because he had "so called" left her and had just finished going through a nasty custody battle to get his kids back. He wanted to come and see me, and I was so excited but still had not learned my lesson from the first time.

When God removes people from your life it is for a reason so you should never go backwards…. but of course, I did.

Laying my eyes on for the first time after 15 years made me happy. All we could do was stare at each other the whole way back from the bus station. He made me believe that we could rebuild and get married.

Now for those who know me, you know that I never wanted to get married (especially after what happened with Keith) and yet here I am contemplating it. While he was with me, I noticed his phone kept ringing constantly. I am not an insecure woman, so I did not think too much of it because I know how break ups go. I just figured that she could not let go and so she kept trying to get him back.

He made it seem like she was just scorned and hurt. I had no reason to doubt him, so I let it be and just enjoyed the time we had together. I saw him off at the bus station and even cried and he said he would call me to let me know he made it back safely.

Once he returned, that's when things changed. The phone calls stopped. There were no more I love you. My first instinct was that something had happened to him because he was going through it. So, I decided to take to Facebook. I tried to send him a message and his page was gone. Out of the blue just disappeared. I then tried to reach him through tagged and then that is where it all became clear to me. He had changed his profile to single and blocked me on tagged.

Upon further investigation, not only did this "ni**a "block me, but I went to the so-called ex's page and low and behold, he had never broken up with this chic. He put her on ice is what he did. Her status said engaged to Stephen.

I was livid! I instantly saw red and was in tears, but it was more anger than anything else. My home girl I worked with at the time was like, "what do you want to do"? The next thing you know, I was in the wind on my way to Raleigh NC with a baseball bat in the trunk. All rational had gone out the window after this b***h started to come for me when I was trying to talk to her like a woman. The way I look at it, he lied to the both of us, so coming after me was a no! The stupid chick had where she worked and the location on her page.

Luckily after about an hour of riding my homie who was trying to talk me down, I was like what if you end up in jail and she and him press charges. You do not know nobody in Raleigh. And all of that would be for what? At the end of the day, he is still going to be with her, and I will be looking stupid. So, then I turned around and went back.

Considering that Stephen and I had a friendship for many years he could have told me the truth. I then would have made my decision to keep it as friends and moved on. But he was selfish and thought only of himself. Moral of this story is, no matter how much history you have with someone and no matter how much you love them that does not mean that they have changed for the better. …..

And now for the grand finale of the mess. I will make this one simple and sweet because he is not even worth the time or space on this entry for me to even include him. Anyway, fast forward to 2017. By this time, I had been celibate for going on 5 years and reconnected with someone from high school who had been incarcerated but had been long time friends throughout middle and high school. Let us call him MAN WHORE.

After he got out, I was the first person he contacted and actually I was kind of surprised until I realized that I had never changed where I moved to on Facebook. He assumed I was still in Tidewater (Virginia) and he told me that he had not too long moved there. He said he was getting ready to go back to work at a local barbershop that his cousin owned. Manwhore was an expert barber.

After endless conversations and plans made, we finally had our encounter. He claimed he had been after me since high school but because he was a lady's man, I always told him he could never have me. We had always remained friends. He told me he wanted for us to work on taking things to another level and that he had to tie up loose ends. He had me really believe that he was serious until he ghosted me not too long afterwards. So, as usual it came to the surface that he was off and on with this chick and was not being honest, with me. I had to cut him loose.

On New Year's Eve of 2021, my inbox was flooded with this chick blowing me up and cussing me out about this fuckin MAN WHORE, so I had to get her together right quick. I let her know that I had not had any dealings with him for months. I told her that I was the one who cut off all communication and to never come into my inbox again with this bullshit. I told her to reach out to the current women he is dealing with. Thus closing this saga forever…..

In conclusion my sisters, never settle, never allow any man to strip you of your value and self-worth and most of all…. LOVE YOURSELF UNCONDITIONALLY!!!!!! Do not be afraid to walk away and protect your peace at all costs.

"I've been in an open marriage that I did not agree to."

—Sound Whisdom

THE DIVINE DIVORCE

By: Sound Whisdom

It is my desire for this letter to be encouraging. It is my desire for my letter to my sister to uplift and inspire you. I even had the idea to write an eloquent "And Still I Rise" type of poem for you, but I need to be transparent about a few things. **I've been in an open marriage that I did not agree to.** The red flags were there, but I didn't know they were red until it was almost too late.

Looking back, I would say that I am the product of an extremely toxic, possibly narcissistic, upbringing. When I say "toxic", I mean derived from one who portrays traits of a "me first"/self-absorbed personality-type that can manifest outwardly or secretly. When I say "toxic", I mean derived from the kind of personality-type that always has you as a source of supply existing only to appease their wants and desires be it physical, mental, emotional, or financial. When I say "toxic", I mean derived from the kind of individual who can blow up your world with extreme love and adoration on the inhale, and then discard you like a filthy rag on the exhale based on figments of their imaginations that may or may not be true. Based on my recent studies about the different aspects of the narcissistic spectrum and toxic personality traits, I can concur that I had a toxic mother, toxic siblings, toxic husbands, boyfriends, friends, and associates. I'm not sure whether or not my father was toxic. When I stand him up against what I do know to be the traits of a toxic person, I'm still straddling the fence in regards to his gambling addiction. He was selfish in a way, but he always made sure my mother had money to pay the bills. He was extremely outgoing, but he always proudly confessed that he was faithful to my mother and had no reason to run around on her. My mother, on the other had, was very strict and calculating.

My mother showed me a tough love, but she made sure that I was clothed, fed, and dedicated to my studies. Some experts suggest that childhood trauma and traumatic events throughout a person's life contributes to the making of a narcissist. My mother lost her mom when she was young and was left to raise her brothers in the midst of an emotionally abusive father. Her husband before she married my father was emotionally abusive as well and even crossed over into physical abuse. Several factors contributed to my mother's narcissism, and it didn't help that her only daughter was "cool as a cucumber". My non-reactionary demeanor set her off every time. She said I was too nonchalant and would demand that I give her an over-the-top response to day-to-day struggles and disappointments. But in the same breath, she made sure I viewed life through rose-tinted glasses. She did her best to shield me from the upsets and evils of the world and reality that existed outside of the world and reality she created for me. She never allowed me the freedom to truly be myself. I had to look and dress a certain way in order to make **her** look good. I was always being showcased as a child. I had to perform, get straight A's, and behave a certain way. I always felt like my parents had me on display. In church I was able to memorize the longest Bible scriptures. I could sing the most complicated songs. I was ALWAYS performing.

Church was my safe space. I accepted the Lord into my life at a very young age. But I was groomed to be sexually broken by an older boy I met in the church. No penetration occurred, but he awakened my sexual curiosity when he would have me sit on his lap and feel me up at the piano when no one was watching. I was a young youth leader still in grade school who knew all the purity chants. But no one was there to hold my hand in accountability. He went on to a Christian college where I visited him on campus one time after sneaking away from a choir performance I had just participated in. He was surprised to see me, but I could tell that his affection had waxed cold. I sat through his ordination a few years later along with my church family, but I was furious that he flipped a switch in me that I couldn't seem to turn off. I was groomed *in* the church, but I learned about sexual perversion *through* the church. Since the world celebrates pre-marital sex, I didn't know how to resist sexual temptation even when it came from my safe space.

I was always looking for acceptance, and as my mother taught me, I performed to get it. I was always figuring out how to please people. So, when I became a teenager, I started noticing cute boys. I started having sex with those cute boys. I even encountered my first toxic romantic relationship with — a cute boy.

I started dating a guy I met in a gospel choir. We met on some teenage, rom-com, fantasy movie-type stuff. We bumped into each other trying to enter the choir room at the same time, and a big cup of soda he was holding wasted on the floor. We locked eyes after dropping to the floor attempting to clean up the mess, and the rest was history. He was highly charismatic. He said that God told him I was going to be his wife even though he ended up being a womanizer. At some point he said to me that he was going to see other women and that I should leave him, but I didn't.

I was mesmerized and dick-matized. This guy was a gifted musician who sang, played the keyboard, played percussion, and could work his way in and out of any conversation. He was a part of the entourage of a popular local pastor and even had a prophetic call on his life. He was masterful at wooing and kept the sex interesting with arranging different venues. My most memorable moment was a theatre space he had access to with plenty of lights, sounds, and action. I was definitely wrapped up in a sexual fantasy with him. Once, we were at his house when his brother caught us and then told his mom. But I still didn't break up with him. We convinced ourselves that we were married in the eyes of God because we were having sex. So, I guess I was his "spiritual wife" and the others were just "something to do". I'm not sure what his thoughts were concerning that whole arrangement, but looking back, I see how desperate I was. Believe it or not, our relationship was supposed to be a testament of purity. It wasn't supposed to be sexual at all. At the beginning of the relationship we'd do these purity tests where he would ask me to put hickies on his neck to prove that we were able to rise above temptation. Epic fail!

Our dark, twisted fantasy of a relationship was "on again and off again" for years. When his dad died in 1994, I gave him some sympathy sex. I got pregnant with his baby, but I wasn't the only one. Two other girls were pregnant with his babies, and I found out because he told me about them. They were all living at his mother's house in Wisconsin, and he wanted me to join them. I was a 16 year old girl from Chicago being propositioned to be a sister-wife in another state. I declined the offer. I found out I was pregnant because I missed my period. My mother knew my cycle, so I had to put fake blood on maxipads and leave them in the trash can to throw her off. My uncontrollable emotions made it hard for me to keep the lie going, so I eventually told her the truth. She cried, and I'm not sure what her response was after her emotions settled. But God saw fit for me to miscarry. The odd fact about the miscarriage is that it happened in the bathroom of my high school after I had gone back to visit my former guidance counselor. All I could hear from the bathroom stall was my former female teachers saying, "It wasn't supposed to happen this way anyway. God didn't need her having no baby at this age." Even after all of that, he wanted me to be the godmother of one of his other children. Of course, I told him no.

After that relationship ended, I was solo until I reconnected with a guy I dated in grade school. By this time, I was turning 17. He took me to see the original *Jumanji* and we had birthday sex in his conversion van. My brother busted in on us once at my parents' house. We stayed together, had a shotgun wedding in December 1996, and gave birth to my first daughter in December 1997. I liked my daughter's father, I even loved my daughter's father, but I'm not sure I was "in love" with him. He was kind, funny, and consistent. He was the perfect "safe choice". We were married for three years altogether. Things changed between us when I was in college. He worked while I went to school, and we were comfortable with that arrangement, so I thought. I was pledging to be a little sister to a fraternity on campus, and I was really into my studies. Our daughter would either be in daycare or be looked after by his mother. One thing I took advantage of while in college was the counseling center.

I went to a campus therapist because I was having problems in my marriage. A major area of concern was in the bedroom. I always wanted to laugh when we had sex, but I couldn't figure out why. *Why is it funny?*

Why can't he ejaculate? What is the problem? When I couldn't satisfy him, I wondered if he was getting sex somewhere else. I couldn't tell if it was me or not. This is when I embarked upon a social experiment. I went exploring, thinking that he was doing the same thing, and I started experimenting with other penises. I cheated on my husband just to compare penises. When I discovered that other penises didn't have a problem with me, I safely determined that **he** was the problem. The therapist ended up leaving the practice before we had a chance to work on my issues, so I was left to fend for myself. I knew that my husband kept a porn collection, so I concluded that maybe he was desensitized. I know for sure that there was no way I could compete with the women in those videos. I felt like he objectified them and wanted me to emulate them. So, as payback for him bragging about his varied sexual encounters prior to me but insisting that he wished I could perform some of his greatest sexual feats, I candidly disclosed my indiscretions.

There was a moment where I tried to stop having the affairs, but I couldn't seem to cut it off. I even suggested a conversion therapy of sorts where I asked him to whip me with a belt in hopes that the pain would force me into a course-correction. It didn't work. I later found out that the rape I experienced in between my last boyfriend and him sent me into a hypersexuality that is common among rape victims. We've had a chance to discuss the happenings of the marriage that eventually ended in divorce. He assures me that I misread the situation with him. He said that he was just happy to have me as his wife and wanted the love-making to last as long as possible. Ultimately, we both realized that neither of us were mature communicators at the time, so lack of communication killed all chances of us working through our problems. I felt that I presented as unkind and selfish in retrospect and that my misread of a situation opened a whole Pandora's Box.

Well, an interesting find recently came to light when a trusted source told me about an item from one of my first ex-husband's collections. He liked to collect things. He took pictures and videos of **everything**. I often feared that the birthing video would end up in the wrong hands. I even feared that one of our sex tapes would get leaked. Well, according to the trusted source, a sex video did get out. The subject matter was said to have been of me and my ex-husband having a sexual encounter. It was stated that we were *anatomical misfits* and that we wouldn't work biologically. I can neither confirm or deny the details of what was on the video, but if the misfit theory is valid, then we were doomed all the way around. Even my mother knew something was off about the marriage.

One day, she was laying on the couch looking at me and said, "I don't know what you're going to do about this husband of yours." "What?!?" I exclaimed. I waited for her to explain her thoughts, but she didn't. She gave me no additional information. Unfortunately, my mother didn't know how to be a positive role model for me when it came to explaining the facts of life. She didn't have a pattern to follow. She was left to figure things out on her own, so she also led me in the same direction. I divorced my husband while I was dating one of my co-workers. He and I were separated at the time but still living together. He started dating someone while we were roommates. So, he had moved on before I did. My co-worker/boyfriend helped me a lot as I was finishing up my Bachelor's majoring in Theatre Arts and minoring in Music. Since I didn't want my married name on my college degree, and my ex asked for his name back on a couple of occasions, I gladly got a divorce. It seemed like a solid business decision to the benefit of all parties involved. My husband had moved out by then and our daughter was four years old when we finalized the divorce. But I had to go back to court one more time because even though the judge said I could resume use of my maiden name, the language of me returning to that name was missing from the divorce decree. Some more money and another filing later, the deed was done.

Unfortunately, my relationship with my co-worker wasn't going in the direction I thought it would go. But why? You might ask. Because... wait for it! He ended up being a schizophrenic and actually crazy. He manifested multiple personalities while we were at work. This was witnessed by myself and several coworkers. All of his personalities had different names, and some were female. He eventually told me that he took pills to kill the personalities when he was in high school, and he thought they were all gone. Obviously, some stayed behind. We dated for three years but needless to say, things didn't work out. After him, I met a guy at an audition. He was charismatic, tall, dark, handsome, and Jamaican. He introduced me to Entrepreneurship, but he was verbally and emotionally abusive. He wanted to restrict my interaction with other people. He would deprive me of sleep because he felt that I needed to be on watch while he did his late night livery service. He wanted me to stay awake during his graveyard work shifts after I'd been doing hair for 12 hours. We were together for five years, and I had to get an Order of Protection against him just to get out of that relationship!

Eventually, I met my two older sons' father. We were together for seven years. We met at a reggae club one night. I was supposed to be meeting someone else, but that guy stood me up. I was a very expressive dancer who loved to dominate the dance floor, and he had that same kind of energy. It intrigued me. And then he called me the next day. He was a single dad. I was a single mom. Our kids got along great (so I thought), so we got together. I had even put together a list of personality traits I wanted in my next mate. I was convinced he met my criteria. He was fun, spiritual, and an empath. But, to my dismay, he too, was narcissistic. He was molding himself to who I was so that I'd be attracted to the likeness. In a sense, he became a male version of me, and I was very comfortable being around "me". The harsh reality of it all revealed it was like being with the same person I dated before but with a different face and a different body.

We were blessed to have two boys together. Based on his own braggadocious conversation he had on speaker phone with our sons one day, he may have a daughter somewhere out there between the ages of our children. I was very sexually accomodating to my second ex-husband, but this joker still had the nerve to sodomize me. I spoke about this incident in my previously published story in *When the Soul Cries Vol. 1: Wife on Paper.* I had to get an order of protection against him too just as I did with "The Jamaican" from my first story. He didn't want to get a psych eval or seek therapy before the divorce. When he filed, he kept changing his mind about what the custody arrangement needed to be. He kept me tied up in divorce court for three years. In the end, he never agreed to anything. The first judge we had died on the bench, and we had to get a new judge who defaulted the case and gave me full custody of our kids. Presently, our sons communicate with their father as often as they can. The parenting time exchange is always interesting but fun. Since our breakup, he has suffered quite a few unfortunate events which resulted in bodily injuries including broken bones and a traumatic brain injury. He had to undergo a psych eval and is now getting treatment for ADHD, anxiety, depression, and the "extra voices" in his head. Time and circumstances seem to have matured us both, and the once bitter friends are now better friends.

Over the course of the three-year divorce drama, I started dating another man, Robert (Rob), with whom I was blessed to have two more children—a boy and a girl. We met at church during choir rehearsal. Actually, I was in the choir but out on leave until the choir president who was also his female best friend called me up and invited me back. Rob had just moved back to Chicago from Texas, and the church was glad to restore him to his position as the minister of music. He started out as a good friend. He helped me out with transportation, and he was really nice to me and my kids. One Sunday, my ailing father walked out of the church; and Rob jumped off the organ, ran outside, and found my dad wandering down the street. He was my savior in so many areas, and I eventually started liking him for more than just a friend. Sooo, one night, I called him on the phone, and said, "I keep hearing your voice in my head, and I can't turn it off." Then he asked me, "So what does a big girl wanna do?" Now, he knew I was married when we met and that my then husband and I had recently separated. Rob had just signed the papers finalizing his divorce as well—this was his third. I assured him that I wasn't in a relationship with my husband and had no desire to return. Maybe that's why he was so accommodating. He told me he could work with that. So, we dated, got engaged, and were finally married on December 19, 2014.

My sons from my second marriage adored Rob and tried to marry me off to him right away. They both voiced their opinions about me needing a new husband early on. My daughter from my first marriage had a cordial relationship with Rob. Yet, she didn't like that he was "all about himself". She didn't like the company he kept or that he smoked weed and cigarettes. Rob hung out with a lot of shady individuals. They would listen to vulgar loud music, curse all day, gossip, talk about sex, and shoot pool. Many of the women were prostitutes, and a lot of the men had gang ties. Rob considered himself like Jesus and Paul of the Bible. But unlike Jesus and Paul, Rob partook of it all. Basically, my daughter felt that he was a hypocrite. She doesn't feel like he lived a life that was true to who he said he was. He called himself a "Christian" but did everything to the contrary. I, on the other hand, she feels made mistakes but kept trying to do better and to truly live according to what I believe. In my observation it all boils down to making a decision to be "church saved" or "Bible-saved". Either way, it seemed that the only way to literally "save our family's life" was to move across country in the middle of a pandemic. We relocated to Texas in June 2020 after our home had been shot up three times between Easter and Father's Day that year.

*****

Looking back, things started going left with Rob when he had a TIA in 2018 which is something like a mini stroke. While he was in the hospital, I went through his phone to see why my radar had been going off lately. I saw flirty text messages he was having with different women, and that bothered me. When I confronted him, he said I was wrong for going through his phone while he was sick. He said that I was kicking him while he was down. Rob eventually explained that sometimes the conversations went too far but that the flirting was harmless. He said that nothing ever happened. He claimed that some of the conversations belonged to his bisexual adult daughter who was living with us at the time and didn't have her own phone. Rob even mentioned that he had let one of his buddies use his phone and some of those conversations were his. When I would find condom wrappers, he would blame it on his friends. He always had a clever explanation as to why it was never him being inappropriate. All of the explanations sounded pretty good and convincing. Each scenario was quite possible, so I decided to let it go. I didn't pursue the accusations any further. That is until I developed a feminine problem at the start of our new life in Texas that just didn't seem to want to go away.

    Things went left with Rob again when he found himself in the hospital in November 2021. This time he was telling a woman on his hospital phone that me and the kids were out of town until Saturday. I was sitting right there next to him. I asked Rob who was on the phone, and he told me. I told him to tell her I said hello, and he did. He was behaving so erratically. I had taken off from work to tend to his medical needs and mine. It was during this time that I got tested at the emergency room one night after Rob basically put me out of his room even though we arranged for overnight privileges. When some of the results came back that night, I found out that I had an STD. Clearly, I didn't give it to myself. I got treated and told his medical staff, but the nurse said his results were negative. Based on my research, false-negative results in men are common—not to mention he'd been on IV antibiotics for seven days before he was tested. To add insult to injury, Rob and his adult daughter tried to turn the tables and blame me for the STD. They said that while I was going back and forth to Chicago for work, I probably cheated, got caught up, and was trying to place the transgression on him instead of taking accountability. Lies, all lies!!! So, there I was dealing with an unrepentant spouse who involved me in an open marriage I did not agree to. I was unsure what my next steps would be, but I know I needed an exit strategy.

    Rob ended up being diagnosed with three different kinds of cancer. During that time, I went on a three-day water-only fast and realized that I'd been in a spiritually, mentally, and emotionally abusive marriage. Although I questioned his behavior at times, he had a clever way of explaining what did or did not happen which made me buy into his reasoning. Once I realized what I was dealing with, I felt like I was in my spiritual right to get a divorce. I attempted to have a virtual consultation with a divorce attorney by phone, but the call never came. I called and emailed letting the office know I was ready for the meeting, but nothing happened. So, there I was sitting in the middle of a park on a bench, just waiting. Then, I started questioning Holy Spirit. *I'm here. What's going on?* Then I heard, *you're looking for a physical divorce, but I'm going to give you a divine divorce.*

I began journaling all the things I was hearing. I thought God was going to provide me with a new husband for Christmas. Not new as in a new person but new as in my husband will be reformed after battling this bout of sickness. I thought God was going to cause him to want to change his ways this time. After all, the girl in the movie got her new husband for Christmas when her old man decided to change his ways. I'm a dreamer and thought for sure my real-life fairy tale would come true.

When Rob got out of the hospital after Thanksgiving, he apologized for involving me in a threesome scenario I agreed to do for one of his birthdays a few years prior. I did that hoping to appease him and to be his flavor. In my eyes the marriage bed had been defiled, but Rob told me that God wouldn't frown upon whatever a married couple agreed to. He had been counseled by a pastor and his wife some years ago who taught that if a married couple decided to have a third party in their bedroom, God wouldn't mind. Since I'd never heard that explanation before, and the idea came from Christian marriage experts, I trusted Rob's lead. I was willing to go with anything that would please my husband, but not for long. After a month of trying to entertain that lifestyle, I called everything off. Anyway, that's all he apologized for. He never apologized for his affiliations back home that almost got me and my kids killed. He never apologized for never praying with me at home or for living a life full of contradiction before our children. He never apologized for his sexcapades or taking our kids on playdates with the "other woman" and her children. He never apologized for smoking weed with minors. He never apologized *for the 14 different women* he was sending sexy text messages to since we had moved to Texas (conversations I found while going through his phone, including pornographic images and videos).

One day, Rob sent me a text message asking me about picking up some condoms that I could use. Under the influence of a messy-boots female acquaintance, I entertained the thought that I really wasn't sure that the message was for me. So, I replied by asking if the message was for me or for one of the other 14 women he was talking to. Then, I ran down all the names of the women I saw in his phone. He assured me that the message was for me, really?!?. Basically, I told him "no" because I had some inner work to do. I needed to free myself from soul ties and to free myself spiritually. It was at that moment that I was convinced of Rob's narcissistic traits. Even his children mentioned he could be selfish, but this truly took the cake. Here he was willing to try and have sex with a "cheating wife" as long as they used condoms she wasn't allergic to. Puh-lease!! I continued to perform the same non-sexual wifely duties I'd been maintaining for months by making sure he ate, had his medication, and made it to his appointments.

My decision was to stay and set firm boundaries which I expressed by making sure Rob had everything he needed for home care, including flying a helper in from Chicago. I set up his medicine tray when he got out of the hospital and made sure there was food in the house. More importantly I informed him that my body was off-limits to him as I took time to heal physically, mentally, emotionally, and spiritually. I slept on the couch while he had the entire master bedroom to himself. The helper and I observed my husband refuse help as he prepared and served his own meal and took his own medicine. I sent the helper back home upon her request, and the adult daughter started complaining that her dad still needed the help. I reported to her that he demonstrated self-sufficiency and that the helper requested to go home.

Over the next few days, I noticed a lot of bloody tissues and mental confusion. The adult daughter sat with him a couple of days and suggested that maybe he needed his blood levels checked. I took my Rob back to the ER on Monday, the 20th of December. He was supposed to do labs and get the biopsy results that day, but he rescheduled the appointment for January 3rd. The entire staff was mortified that he did that, but they explained that he needed to stay at least one night so they could find out what just made him spike a fever. He agreed to stay and was immediately swabbed for COVID, flu, and RSV. COVID came back positive. Basically, the nosebleeds were a part of the blood cancer in his body that was preventing his blood from clotting properly. The COVID infection is what caused his confusion.

The COVID started off as mild but quickly took a turn because of his compromised immune system. He received his vaccine back in June, but he still contracted the disease. His body fought as best as it could, and the medical professionals did everything they could to support his life function. I was able to minister to him at his bedside and say a prayer for repentance that I hope he was able to repeat in his mind. I even ministered in song to him on Christmas day. With his adult daughter at his bedside later that night, I was able to have the children say their expressions of love through video call before the hospital removed the final life supports. The daughter said she held his hand and played Kirk Franklin's "The Storm is Over Now." He made his transition at 12:59am on December 26, 2021. I mentioned to the daughter that Rob shared with me that if anything ever happened to him, he only wanted to be on life support for 6 days. The daughter pointed out to me that he got his wish because he didn't want to go back to the hospital anyway. The hospital admission and everything that happened from December 20-26 totaled six days worth of life support. The very support I was seeking for my life was that of a "life-saving divorce"—hopefully yielding a multifaceted renewal of some sorts. Solemnly, I am now the recipient of the *DIVINE DIVORCE* of death which has ushered me into the "Widow's Club".

*****

The timeline of Rob's passing was very unusual. While I was going through the process of discovering my own spiritual awakening, dealing with his sickness, and then coping with his passing, I joined quite a few online support groups. Narcissistic abuse support group, check! Cancer support group, check! Caregivers with Children support group, check! Grieving wives support group, check! I was desperately trying to understand the world in which I was now living. Once Rob died, I looked to my faith community and not his (what he told them is a story for another book). I finally began to understand the trauma I had just escaped. I found an online community led by a woman who divorced her narcissistic husband and escaped from a Christian cult. She is now a life and trauma therapist. She teaches the women in her group to use the same trauma-based tools she learned in her training and in her own life to rid themselves of the physiological existence of the damage that the trauma has caused. I wish I had a purity community that taught me about relationship traps all those years ago. I wish I knew how to set boundaries and, more importantly, how to keep them.

My Sister, it is essential to learn what triggers you. The next step is to create and keep your boundaries around those triggers. Protect your peace at all costs! Boundaries will naturally send the unwanted people in your life through the process of elimination. It's scary because you don't know what's coming, and I had no idea death was coming to my door. I thought I'd be a divorcee in the literal or figurative sense, but definitely not a widow. God gave me a divine divorce, and I will be careful to take my time to heal and help my children heal. I love to learn, and have cherished my classes for helping me feel some sense of normalcy. My classes span theology, evangelism, and worship arts and have all helped me to reset myself with each stage of grief that unfolds. What's even more intentional has been my quest to find the best spiritual community for the children and I in this season of our lives. Fortunately, we are now at home in One Community Church "where no one walks alone".

Sister, do not self-identify with what other people think of you. Obtaining your self-identity from within helps, but sometimes the *inner-me* is an *enemy* shaped by past hurt and disappointments. The best confidence booster is seeing yourself through the eyes of the One who created you—The Great I Am, The Living God. I believe in Jesus, who gave His life for my freedom, so I gladly believe in what God says about me. I am fearfully and wonderfully made!

*****

I am excited about my fresh start and a new beginning as a widowed mother. I hope to start an LLC in Texas so I can have a family business to create generational wealth. I have a robust community of support, and my children and I are well on our way to mental wellness and healing. Right now, I'm living the "Preferred Life" as a single and will pay close attention to the teachings of my pastor, Dr. Conway Edwards. In his

"Solo to Soulmate" series he shared a list of ten points I wish I knew in my teen years. Well, it's never too late to learn, Sis, and I am honored to have his permission to share a summary of those nuggets with you now:

"10 Red Flags to Look Out for in a Relationship" Proverbs 27:17

1. You and/or your current partner started dating without getting over the ex partner.
2. When you feel like you just have to be in a relationship and cannot stand to be single.
3. When you see the other person as a project that can be fixed by marriage.
4. When you let your sex organs attract you to them instead of letting their character speak.
5. When others around you in your family and friendship circles don't celebrate the relationship because of red flags they see.
6. When your safety feels threatened mentally, emotionally, physically, or spiritually.
7. When your partner has more opposite sex friends than same sex friends.
8. When there is an extremely overwhelming showering of love and affection only in the beginning of the relationship.
9. When in conflict they shut down, can't admit wrongs, and/or shift the blame.
10. When you are trying to get from them what ONLY God can give you to make you feel whole.

I AM THE BREAKER

By: Lenora Jones Elliott

I was listening to a mini sermon and the young lady who was ministering to the church said that we have to declare that, "I AM The Breaker!

Give God glory for your vision- give him glory for your purpose because he is about to use you in your situation to help someone else. There are some other people who are in / were in the same situation that you are in right now, but they didn't make it. You are in the place right where you are right now…because God is gonna use you to bring those who feel like they can't make it…He's gonna bring them OUT!"

This truly ministered to my spirit. For the last few weeks I have been having my own struggle with a few things, but one issue in particular has been consuming my thoughts, mind and prayers. And wouldn't you know it….as I am going thru a few friends/ sisters started calling me who are dealing with the same issue.

At first I copped out! Yep…I looked for an escape…my response to them was…"I'm not the one, because apparently, I can't get it right either!" BUT God has been ministering to me and sending messages to me to assure me that I am going thru for a reason. This is my Training Ground…My "AIT"- my Advanced Individual Training! (the training in the military that comes immediately after basic training, where you concentrate on your future position/assignment)

I heard a minister say that your Misery is often your Ministry! Let me just tell you that "relationships" issues have been my misery for years…and wouldn't you know it…it's truly my calling and I haven't been able to see it for what it is until now! God has truly been speaking to me and dealing with me to the point where now I can't just be complacent anymore!

Know that, like any good parent God wants the best for you. But you have to make some decisions regarding your present state. First you must take it to GOD! If there is something that's stopping you from moving into your destiny…GIVE IT TO HIM!

Then you Must Exercise Faith- you must believe that God has Greater for you. When we settle…when we become comfortable with where we are… we hinder our own walk/ministry/destiny! Often we don't press completely thru because we fear the outcome…We can no longer give in to the Fear of failing…falling….disappointing….or being rejected!

The Key is to Let God fix it!

If you are anything like me, you've been trying to deal with the issue plaguing you right now, trying to fix it within your own might by yourself! That's not the answer! Because as we wrestle with the issue(s) and/or the situation(s), the enemy continues to bombard us.

When the enemy sets his sights on you, the attacks become greater in number…mightier in force and (in the words of my sister Jennifer, the intensity is multiplied "to the 10th power"!

So trust me when I tell you that, it REALLY is as simple as turning it over to God, believing that He Has Your back, and doing what He has instructed you to do. When you do this and start walking this thing out, the enemy will no longer have your mind, he will no longer stop you from moving into your destiny by keeping you in your past!

KNOW that You were in that Place for a Purpose. God's calling you to purpose because You are the Breaker!

It's time to Break those generational curses! It's time to break those things that others spoke over your life.

You Just might have to OPEN YOUR MOUTH AND DECLARE (out loud) "I AM THE BREAKER"!

Those curses…those ties …those chain that had you in bondage… speak to them and declare that it stops with you…TODAY!

No longer will they have an effect on you, your family, our household or your destiny!

I AM THE BREAKER

You have the Power to block attacks designed to take out your children, your children's children, your finances, your relationships…, your marriage, your walk and Your Destiny!

You already possess it, you just gotta use it. Don't worry about not feeling equipped, don't worry about feeling like you are not quite sure how to do this. Do not allow fear to paralyze you. Let me help you, the answer is in your Mouth! Greater is He who is in me, than he who is in the world!

I challenge you to speak this one sentence over your life, make this declaration out loud and then witness the manifestation of God's Glory!

Declare that … I AM The Breaker!

Speak it into existence and then walk into your destiny!

You are Great…You just gotta see what I see in you…and Believe what God has already declared for you!!!

"He was my soulmate...when you lose someone you have that kind of connection with, the grieving process can take years to recover from."

*– **Nikki***

IT COMES IN WAVES
By: Nikki Duncan Talley

September 25, 2021, marks 25 years of marriage to my husband. Before you get excited and congratulatory in your mind, let me be honest with you; I wish my marriage was over. In fact, I wish it had never even started. I had no idea what I was getting myself into. The moral fiber of my mindset and his wasn't compatible. I can't help but think, *how the f*** did I get here?*

My husband and I met in 1999 when I was attending school at Catawba College in Salisbury, North Carolina. I was also *engaged* when we met. We became friends and remained that way for a year. My fiancé at the time was in the US Army when I received the news that he'd gotten a girl pregnant. I **refused** to be a stepmother, so I ended the engagement. He and I maintained a friendship until his death in 2014.

Before I move too fast, let me start from the beginning...

I met my ex-fiancé as a freshman in high school. During my freshman year, I chose to enroll in ROTC to avoid going to Bayside High School. I wanted to go to Princess Ann instead. Nevertheless, ROTC is where he and I met. One day we went to a naval academy game where it was the Navy vs. the Army. He and I paired up and were joint at the hip the entire time. On the way back to school, we kissed.

I had no idea he was dating one of my friends. She heard about the kiss between us and confronted me about it. I don't like feeling upset and confrontation is not my thing. I never wanted to be in a position where I could hurt someone. I also wasn't interested in fighting over a boy, but I was more than able to defend myself if she touched me. And I let her know that. She sat down and quickly determined he wasn't worth the fight.

He and I, however, remained friends and began dating during our sophomore year of high school. We were the quintessential high school sweethearts. We went to prom together. Our families were acquainted and went on vacations together. Our families are still relatively close. His mother is like a second mother to me and I treated his sister as if she was my own. He and I dated until our senior year in high school. We broke up because his mother felt that my presence was affecting his grades. She also felt like I had more control over his life than she did, so she didn't want us seeing each other.

So he and I both dated other people our senior year. Although we weren't "together," he was still at my house every day after school. We didn't attend senior prom together, but he came to my house after prom, and we went out with some friends for a late-night breakfast.

My mother couldn't understand why we weren't together. She didn't know why we were dating other people if we were always hanging out with one another. We got back together right before he went to boot camp for the Army and I was off to college at Catawba.

* * * * *

It's 1998, and we kept in touch via phone calls and letters. I attended his Army graduation not long before Christmas break. We were both back home for the holidays and it felt like old times. Every year on Christmas day, we had a tradition of going to his uncle's house for a family dinner. Only this Christmas would be slightly different this year. He proposed to me in front of his family that Christmas. But it didn't come as a surprise. I knew he'd gone to my family previously and asked them if it was okay that he proposed to me. So I knew it was coming. Of course, I said, "yes."

He was deployed to Korea shortly after. Army soldiers cannot bring their families to Korea because it's a 1-year duty station. Whether we got married right away or waited, I wouldn't be able to go. The summer of my sophomore year in college, I told him, "I heard that the first year of marriage is the hardest year of marriage, and I don't want to be a million miles away from you in the hardest year of marriage."

1999 rolls around. I guess I didn't have a choice because he went to Korea, and I went back to school. He and I were good for quite some time.

Or so we thought. In hindsight, things weren't that great because we were both cheating on one another. Neither of us knew it at the time. I never got caught because I never got pregnant, but I couldn't say the same for him. He'd gotten a girl pregnant in Korea. One day, he called to break the news to me.

There was really no point in cheating. He was my first *everything*. I was just young, in college, and there were a lot of hot guys at my school. I had a lot of male friends and I worked for the athletic department. All the guys knew I was engaged. I led with that until I met a guy named CJ. He was absolutely gorgeous. I was infatuated with his body and the fact that he was an upperclassman interested in *me*. We studied together until it became a little more than studying. Although I was cheating, I was never in another *relationship*. All of my bouts of cheating were just me passing the time.

In my junior year in college, my fiancé called me. "I have something I need to tell you. I got this girl pregnant. I don't know what to do."

He and I had grown up together, so we were always really good friends. Here was a guy that I was planning on spending the rest of my life with on the other end of the phone telling me that he'd gotten someone else pregnant. It seems odd that he told me so easily and casually. What's more mind-boggling is the audacity to ask me what **he** should do. *Wait... somebody's pregnant?* I thought to myself.

"What the f*** do you mean?" I blurted out. "This isn't going to work."
So we were supposed to get married and take care of his kid with someone else? No. That wasn't the plan. I knew him *very* well. I knew he was going to be an excellent father. We were both 20-year-old. I understood that trying to be a step-parent at that time in my life wouldn't work out well.

"I'm not sure what you're gonna do."

"I f***** up. This wasn't supposed to happen. I told her that I didn't wanna have a baby with her and that we're supposed to get married."

"Looks like that's not gonna happen now," I stated. I was clear that this wasn't the way I wanted to enter into marriage with him, and I wasn't going to bend on that.

He wasn't playing me. We were cheating on each other. I just didn't get caught. The difference between him and I was he had to take on a responsibility that I didn't have to.

*****

So now it's the year 2000 and I had to let him go. We broke up. I received a phone call at 5 a.m., a ridiculous hour for anyone to be calling. He called to tell me that the girl wanted to keep the baby, so he proposed to her. They were engaged. But she lost the baby, however, the wedding was already scheduled. As I listened to him, I realized he didn't know what to do, *again*. He was looking for advice from me. **I was still heartbroken.**

My then-boyfriend, now husband, was lying next to me in the bed when I received that phone call.

"I don't care what you do. I don't have to wake up next to that person for the rest of my life, and currently, I'm in bed with my boyfriend, so I will talk to you later." I hung up the phone.

I was being mean and nasty to him because I wanted him to feel some of the heartbreak that I was feeling.

I was also told that she knew about me. They ended up getting married and she became pregnant shortly after. He told her that she needed to befriend me somehow because if they were ever going to work, she needed to understand I would always be in his life **forever.**

I didn't want to be her friend! What would make him think that I would be friends with the woman he cheated on me with and married? That about sums up my junior year of college.

I continued with my schooling in 2001. My boyfriend and I continued dating for a while. We broke up, and after graduation, I met Jared through a mutual friend from school. He and I hit it off. We had a lot of similar interests and began dating casually. He took me home to meet his parents and grandparents, but I wasn't ready to introduce him to my family.

Around my birthday and homecoming, I went back to my college. My ex-boyfriend, now husband, was still there playing football. My ex and

I messed around the weekend of my birthday, and by December, I was pregnant. I was also *still* dating Jared.

When I found out about the pregnancy, I told Jared. I revealed to him it wasn't his baby based on the timeline of my pregnancy. Jared didn't care. "That's fine. We can still be together. I will take care of the baby as if it's my own."

Here's the problem with that: Jared was a white guy. There was no way we could pass this off as *his* baby. I didn't want to be *that girl*. You know, the pregnant girl in the delivery room whose baby comes out looking so different that anyone looking at the baby would know it wasn't "the father's." To have to explain that to our families would've been unfair to both of us. Jared still didn't care and was very upset when I told him that I wouldn't do that. That was too risky, destructive, and irresponsible.

Jared had abandonment issues which I wasn't prepared to deal with long-term. When he was 12-years-old, his mother cheated on his father with his father's best friend. She came back into his life when he was 21-years-old. He needed a lot of validation from me. He needed confirmation that he was always doing or saying the right things. He was insecure and needed reassurance of **everything.** I didn't understand why anyone needed another person to 'okay' their every move. His needs were overwhelming for me at that age.

I broke things off with Jared and he wasn't happy. When the relationship was over, I realized that he was more serious about me than I was about him. I've taken low-level psychology classes in the past, so I know that his mother leaving him as a child affected how he related to and operated with women. I never sat back and thought about the 'whys' of that relationship until I was older. He was a really good guy; he just needed the kind of care that I couldn't provide.

I wound up living back at home and telling my parents that I was pregnant in 2002. When I arrived home, my ex-fiancé, his wife, and their baby had moved into his mother's house. When he found out that I was home and pregnant, he and the baby would come to my house every afternoon. The baby played while he and I talked. Shortly after that, he was discharged from the Army. That was the dumbest thing I'd ever heard.

I remember that he planned to do 20 years in the service, retire and start another career at 38 years old. I told him that just because he and I were no longer together didn't mean his plan needed to change.

My mother told me that when he first came home, he visited her and my stepfather. She said she asked him where his wife was and he told her she was sitting in the car.

"Have you lost your mind? Don't you ever do that again!"

She told him to invite her in, keeping in mind that although he and I were engaged to be married, and things went left, our families were still friends.

He went back into the military and I didn't know where he was stationed. Life went on.

*****

I gave birth to my daughter in 2003. Her father was there for her delivery, even though we weren't together. I didn't want to be in a relationship with him, and I was clear with him about that. I stayed in Virginia for quite some time. My ex-fiancé and I never actually lost contact. Apparently, his marriage was rocky when we reconnected and started dating again. I was living in Charlotte, NC, and he was stationed in Virginia at Fort Eustis. He'd drive to Charlotte to pick me up and my daughter would stay in Charlotte with her aunt or grandmother.

My daughter's father was under the impression that we were in a relationship because we had a baby together. We were spending time together with our child, and that's probably what gave him that idea. But I wasn't under that impression. I was dating my ex-fiancé.

One day, my ex-fiancé was driving down to Charlotte to pick me up. My daughter's aunt came to pick her up for the weekend. My daughter's father found out that I didn't have the baby. He knew I'd be at my apartment alone, so he popped up. I told him I was on my way out and that he should leave. He was pissed off, but he left.

My ex-fiancé and I drove up to Chesapeake and went to the movies. I remember it like it was yesterday; we saw Fahrenheit 9/11. We stayed the

IT COMES IN WAVES

night together and hung out in Charlotte the next day. We weren't intimate consistently. We went through periods when we didn't have sex and times that we did.

He got stationed in Arizona, but he and I still kept in contact. We saw each other off and on until 2007. Later the same year, I started having severe migraines that caused visual impairment. I went to the neurologist to get checked out. The neurologist told me that she believed the migraines were coming from stress. I had recently lost my stepfather in 2006 and my grandmother in 2007. That may have been too heavy a load for my body to process. So I decided I needed a change of scenery. My daughter was 4-years-old. I applied for jobs in other states and got a phone call from Texas Woman's University. They flew me out for an interview, and I got the job. I packed up and drove to Texas. My mother was taking care of my daughter while I was getting settled in.

My ex-fiancé and I were still in contact. He told me about a girl he was dating who was in the Navy. In 2008, she got pregnant and they decided to get married. How, when he was still married to his first wife? His new fiancé chose to pay for him to file for divorce from the first wife so that they could get married.

We kept in contact. We checked on each other. I always contacted him on his birthday. One day, my daughter's father came to visit me and our daughter. At the time, he was in the Air Force Reserves but injured his ankle while working on base. So he was being discharged from the military. When he came to Texas, he told me, "I want my family. I want us to be together." The whole spiel.

I worked at the University and lived on campus in an apartment. He couldn't stay in my campus apartment if we weren't married. He didn't think it was a bad idea to get married. I figured, *why not?* I mean, we already had a kid together, so I decided to try to make it work. We got married on September 25, 2008.

We stayed in Texas until February 2009. We moved back to Virginia and no one knew that we'd gotten married. I hadn't even told my mother. The only person that knew was my ex-fiancé. We stayed with my mother when we went back to Virginia.

"Y'all can't stay here if you're not married," My mother told us.

"It's okay. We're already married," I revealed.

My mother was stunned. She said she didn't think we would get together or stay married.

"Oh, we'll be okay," I reassured her. I would make sure of it because failure wasn't an option. But things weren't okay. They never were.

It wasn't that we grew up in different cities. We came from different **worlds.** My parents had been divorced for a very long time. But I had two sets of parents and two sets of grandparents. I had a huge family. I had my biological parents and their family and my step-parents and their family.

Meanwhile, there were a lot of things about my husband's upbringing that I didn't know until we were married. You find out a lot more about a person when you become a part of their inner circle. For example, I didn't know that his father was married to another woman when he was conceived. He also had a half-brother that was 11 months older than him. His mess of a childhood made it hard for him to be an actual partner for me.

Anybody who knows me knows that I don't bite my tongue very often. But there have been many times that I've bitten my tongue while in arguments with my husband because I'm aware that some words spoken aloud can't be taken back and can be very damaging. I do love my husband, so I would never want to hurt him. But there are times when I struggle with my true feelings. I can't just say what I want.

In the past, my husband and I have gotten into arguments, and he's mentioned things that still sit in the back of my mind. He'd say something like, "I don't know what a good relationship looks like." I'd always think to myself, *I know, because I'm dealing with the effects of it.*

When you move from one state to another, people typically do things like get a job. My husband has no problem allowing me to be the one that carries most of the financial weight. I do it to make sure that he and I don't fail ourselves, fail our daughters, or fail our family. I want more for my children. In order to make sure our family could make ends meet, I've closed out multiple retirement packages that I had and sacrificed a lot, whereas he's done almost nothing.

I hate failing and I hate to see others fail. I'll go through a great deal to ensure that I don't fail and do my best to help save someone else from failure. But that's an unrealistic pattern of thought. Failure is a part of life. Often, it propels us to the place where we're supposed to be. Give yourself some grace to unlearn the thought process of being afraid to fail and the god complex of trying to save everyone else.

His financial lack made it easy for me to move like I was a single woman. My ex and I got back in contact and one thing led to another. The affair started with a kiss and carried on from 2012-2014. For the most part, we had always kept in contact. But that kiss brought all the feelings back. Occasionally we had mind-blowing sex when we saw one another, but we talked a lot about our marriages and our concerns. We both felt like the lives we were living weren't the lives we were supposed to be living. We wanted to be together, but we couldn't just divorce our spouses to get married. So we made a pact that we would give our marriages one last try, and if things didn't work, we would move forward with our plan to be together.

My husband felt like he knew something was going on, and he was right. But I refused to confirm his suspicion. I wasn't ready for that kind of trouble. So I purposely gaslit the entire situation. I made him believe he was wrong and made up everything in his mind.

* * * * *

It is 2014 and I was on a hiatus from Facebook and didn't see all of the notifications of people tagging me in different events and happenings. I decided to take a trip home to see my family. I stopped at my ex's mother's house and his sister was there. She said she was trying to contact me via Facebook to tell me that my ex was killed the night before in a motorcycle accident. The news didn't register through my brain immediately. It took me a minute to process the words. I couldn't believe it. Everything had changed. I didn't have my best friend anymore and the possibility of us one day being together was done.

A couple of days before the funeral, my ex's sister, her boyfriend, and I were sitting down having a drink.

"I know your husband is thinking, *thank God for small favors*," His sister told me.

"Christina, please! Don't say that."

"What? It's *my* brother. I know the kind of relationship y'all had. I'm just saying that because I'm sure your husband is like, *I don't have to deal with him ever again in life*."

I guess she meant, a dead person can't take your husband or wife. She thought my husband felt relieved that my ex would no longer be in the way. Maybe he did.

In the days that followed, the military had a memorial service for him at Fort Bragg. His mother insisted I ride to the service with the family, so I did. His wife didn't. His mother wanted me to sit on the front row with her, but I *couldn't* do that. The last thing I needed was a spectacle at his memorial. I sat directly behind her, and his sister sat next to me. His wife strolled into the memorial late in what could only be described as a long, wife-beater of a dress.

Christina and I kept it together. We knew he wouldn't want us at the memorial service acting a fool. When the military does a memorial for an active service member, they do a last roll call at the end. A roll call is when one service member calls out the names of everyone with the same rank and in the same unit as the service member who has passed away. Everyone in attendance whose name is called says they're present. When they called his name Christina and I cried.

His wife was hysterically sobbing. His 5-year-old son looked at her and yelled out for her to be quiet, twice. Instantly his sister and I stopped crying because we almost burst into laughter.

During the ride back home, I asked Christina, "why didn't she ride with the family?"

"We don't like her," She told me plainly.

I also found out that his mother was his beneficiary over everything. His wife didn't even have the privilege of deciding what would happen to his body or where he would be buried, which was odd. They'd been married for a while. By then, she should've had *some* say so.

When he and I were younger, I told him that he needed to protect his assets. Although we weren't married, he wanted to make me his beneficiary, and I told him not to do that. I don't think he would've ever changed that, and given the way things went, that would've posed a problem later on.

When it came time for the actual funeral, my husband decided he wanted to attend with me. I never asked him to go. I couldn't understand why he'd want to go. I told him that there was no way I would attend the funeral with him if the tables were turned.

He told me, "I've spoken to him before."

I stood there, "you spoke to him before?"

I guess he thought that because he had a previous conversation with my ex, he was entitled to be there. Whatever. I let him accompany me.

My ex's mother offered for me to ride to the funeral with the family again, but I chose not to. That would've been going too far this time. When my husband and I arrived at the funeral, my ex's cousins were outside waiting for the family to arrive. One of them yelled, "Nikki! I knew you would be here!"

"Yes, and this is my husband." I had to make sure everyone was in step because I didn't need the drama.

Granted, I've known this family since I was 13-years-old. But no matter what was going on between me and my husband, I didn't want him to feel uncomfortable. Yet, I could not fathom how he felt comfortable inserting himself in this situation anyway. I mean, this was *my ex-fiancé*. I don't know how that works.

One of my ex's cousins pulled me to the side and informed me that he didn't look like himself in the casket. He passed away on May 10, 2014. The funeral didn't happen until May 20, 2014. The military isn't the best when it comes to makeup on dead folk. She was preparing me for what I was about to see. My husband sat near the back of the chapel while I went to say my final goodbye.

About 15 feet from the casket, I stopped. I couldn't walk any further. The only thing I could think about was him not looking like himself and me passing out at the casket. How would that look? The optics. So I sat down and talked to his grandmother. She looked at me and said, "I knew you would be here. My grandson loved you so much." I thought, *that's a bit much grandma.* Thank God my husband wasn't standing there.

I couldn't walk past the casket, so I went back to my seat. I never saw him in the casket. I don't think I could handle it. I went to sit next to my husband. After the funeral, we went to the gravesite where the military performed the 21 gun salute. They folded the flag, presented it to his family, and lowered the casket. As we were walking away, his wife approached me. "I wanted to come and thank you for taking care of my mother and sister-in-law because I know you and him were…" She held this *really* pregnant pause.

"Friends." I finished her sentence.

"Yea, friends." She was trying to cause drama while my husband was standing right there.

She walked away and his sister walked up to me.

"I would hate to have to drag her at this funeral."

"Chrissy, it's alright. Don't worry about it. I don't know what she was trying to do, but we're talking about a dead man now." No need for the bullsh*t.

I went to the repass with my husband in tow. My husband and one of my ex's cousins (whom we were really close with when we were young) stood outside and talked for a while. All in all, it wasn't as awkward as I thought it would be. When I look back on all this, my ex was such a large part of my teenage and young adult life that I wouldn't be the same friend, mother, daughter, or wife without his presence. I wouldn't be the same person I am without some of the richness he brought to my life.

I can't say that I'm glad or relieved, but I don't think I would've made it through his death if we had left our spouses to be with each other. **He was my soulmate.** I don't think there will ever be another person with whom I have that deep connection. When you lose someone you have that kind of connection with, the grieving process can take years to recover from. The grieving process is not quick by any means. **It comes in waves.** I still have his number saved in my phone. Some things have happened in my life, since his death, that I usually would've called him and told him about. Not because I felt like he was my soulmate, but because he was my good friend. Those are the times when I feel the weight of his death. **It hits hard.**

Throughout our relationship, he's been stationed near and far. It wasn't uncommon for us to go through periods of minimal communication. Sometimes we'd go a couple of years without seeing each other. We didn't have day-to-day contact, and that was normal. But when I have big moments in my life, when his birthday passes, or I see the Brooklyn Nets are doing well, I go through these moments alone because I realize I can't call him and share those moments with him.

The truth of the matter is, my ex had my loyalty. I was his wife without being his wife. My husband acquired the comfort of being with me. I wasn't as transparent in my relationship with my husband as I should've been in the past. I gave my husband mixed signals. I take full ownership of the decisions I made. To anyone caught in the middle of two people, make sure that one relationship is closed before you enter into another one.

One day, I asked my husband if he thought we would've gotten married regardless of the Texas situation pushing us to do so. He said yes, but I disagree. He said that he wanted to marry me because he loved me and wanted to be a family. But I got married because it was the requirement to keep him in close contact with our daughter. My husband wasn't a huge part of my daughter's life for the first five years of her life. So I wanted her to have him around. I did what I thought was right at the time. My decision wasn't malicious. Eight years ago, my oldest daughter said to me, "if y'all didn't have us, you wouldn't be married to daddy." She was ten years ago at the time. I have no idea what would make her say that. But I keep that memory tucked. Adults make the horrible decision of staying in a relationship **knowing** it is not a good idea. Please, don't stay in a relationship for your children. If you're not in love with that person, why waste everybody's time? If you would still be with that person whether or not children were involved, then you know you're in the right place.

Things happen exactly how they're supposed to. Our lives are intricately designed. Sometimes we think we took the wrong path. I don't think anything is by chance. The mistakes, the failures, and the poor choices all work for our good. I feel that it's all designed to get us where we're supposed to be, operating fully in our purpose.

*"People will pass judgment regardless if you hide the truth or live a lie, so **LIVE YOUR TRUTH**."*

–Lakeisha

ACKNOWLEDGING THE VOID

By: LaKeisha Wilson

I grew up with just my mother and sisters, my father wasn't around consistently. To my knowledge, my sisters and I had the same father. I knew I always felt different or that there was something missing, but I was not enlightened enough to consider there was a "void". I would later learn the reason for the emptiness I felt from time to time would eventually be revealed and explained.

Around my 20th birthday, I answered the call to the ministry. In that same year I discovered that who I thought was my biological father wasn't my father after all. My mother wanted me to meet *this preacher to discuss my call* and told me there was a reason, but I didn't think much of it initially. Sometime after we met, one day the Holy Spirit began speaking to me about my family, father, and that preacher I met. (I didn't recognize it to be the Holy Spirit at that time, but soon learned and understood His voice) God revealed to me that day, that that preacher I met was my father. I couldn't rest after that startling revelation, and, apparently, neither could my momma. The next morning, we were both up before 6 am. I was up earlier ironing and preparing for my day when she walked in the room and started talking. I remember at some point she had me stop ironing and sit down. At that point in my listening to her pour out I knew what she was about to say. What she finally revealed to me was confirmation. The preacher she introduced me to was my father. I told her that the Holy Spirit had already revealed that to me the day before. She looked relieved. **We hugged and cried together.**

My parents had an affair. My mother didn't go into great detail when she told me her side of the story. She did explain she was going through challenges in her marriage with my sister's father, so she confided in her pastor for spiritual counseling. One thing led to another and....well...you know the rest. My assumption is that it was not a lengthy affair but a one-time encounter of which I am the product.

It took some processing to forgive my mother for the deception. For 20 years, I was led to believe my father was a different person. She explained her reasons for not telling me. What I found out was she hadn't told **anyone**. Not a soul, for 20 years! It was my understanding, that part of why she kept this truth a secret was to protect the church. There was speculation and a lot of gossip about who my father was, but no one addressed her directly about it. Not even my assumed father or the biological one.

It didn't take me long to forgive her because I understood her viewpoint and strength. I understood that she was in a difficult position and had to make a decision. She said with all she went through during her pregnancy with me, she could have lost her mind. But it was the pregnancy that kept her sane. She knew that my life was dependent on her. It was easier to forgive her when I understood her struggle and admired her strength.

I had an equal amount of resentment for both of my parents. I chose not to blame one parent more than the other. Occasionally I had human moments about my dad and this situation. I seldomly vented to my friends about it. Most of the time I vented in prayer. My father never directly apologized for his absence in my life, but he did express his gratitude and love for me. When I was ready I slowly began to try and build a relationship with this man. Doing so felt weird, complicated, and awkward. But all in all, I realized that neither my assumed father nor my biological father defined me. I knew my worth and identity is found my Heavenly Father.

More than 10 years after starting to build a relationship with him, I started feeling a tug at my spirit to call or visit my biological father more often than I had been doing. But I ignored the thoughts and feelings to do so. I was grateful to be able to visit or speak with him. But in reality it was work to really form a bond and there was still an emptiness and awkward feeling no matter what we did or how often we would visit. Therefore avoiding him also meant not dealing with the void that really wasn't getting filled with our visits. With all that I was dealing with at that time in my life I simply chose not to give the relationship my energy and ignored that tug at my spirit.

But one day I got a phone call I couldn't ignore. A family member told me that he'd been in an accident and believed he needed someone to help care for him or to go to a nursing home. This news was hard to believe and accept. By this time, many knew I was his daughter. There was another family member in the picture who previously was taking on the role of a daughter to him, but shortly after I came into the picture, she stepped back. Apparently she had more than enough on her plate. It seemed like she wanted us to formulate a bond and was glad for me to take over all the responsibilities she had taken on to aid him.

He had been divorced from his second marriage for several years when I began to help him before eventually becoming his primary care taker. Although he has a son (adopted from his first marriage), I am his only biological child. Yet with him and all other family there was, there was no one else providing him with the help and support he needed. So I stepped up as if I felt called or obligated to. I did all I could to care for him without placing him in a facility. There were times when I was angry and hurt because no one was volunteering to help me provide the care he needed aside from my husband. I felt alone in it and wished for more support from a family I really didn't know. I wished I could've done more for him, but I had to protect my peace, take care of myself, and be there for my husband and kids. The decline in his health and the toil of traveling daily became too much. All other options failed and I had to place him in a nursing facility. I rarely knew if any of his family (my family I didn't really know) were visiting him because there was only one who really communicated with me consistently. His health further declined. Just as I had feared, he was gone less than 2 years later. I'll never forget the call from the nursing home informing me of his passing.

In his last years, he began losing some mental capacity at times. He was well enough to answer a particular question I had. As I drove him to an appointment one day, I asked him about his reasoning for keeping his distance from me. He knew there was a possibility that I could be his child, but he made the decision not to pursue the truth. He told me that he was married and in ministry. My perception of his answer was that because he was in ministry, he couldn't embrace the truth and live it because that would've meant exposing himself and jeopardizing his reputation. Yet my mother perceived that when she revealed to him that she was certain I was his child, he was heartbroken. I believe he felt regret because of all those years of lost time.

My only regret is that I didn't dig deeper into forming a closer relationship before he passed. I wished I had more time with him to have talked about life, asked him more questions, talked about God, his childhood more, his call to ministry, or just any and everything. There was so much knowledge and wisdom in him that I didn't tap into. I've made my peace with what I do know about the situation. I have no desire to dig up anything else about it as all is forgiven. However, I think my mother has had to forgive herself several times. We often go through traumatic experiences and think we've fully healed from them until something else bubbles up, and we have to forgive ourselves again. Sis, forgive yourself as many times as you need to. Take time to acknowledge your experiences for what they are even if they reveal some uncomfortable truths.

My truth is that in all the 21 years of a relationship with a father who was assumed my biological father (who died when I was 21) and 16 years of relationship with my true biological father, there was still a void. The lack of connection and inconsistency I experienced with them both showed me who my *real* father is: God. With each father or even father figure I've had in my life **NONE** have fathered me like God. It has taken me a long time to recognize and acknowledge that void that I have had for years. At the same time, I didn't *feel* it until I was forced to pay attention to my thoughts about what a father is supposed to be. In caring about, observing, and criticizing my husband, the father of my children and his relationship with them; I recognized in my experience with a father, there was a void. When I grieve the loss of my father I also grieve experiences in the relationship that I never had the chance to have. I grieve the relationships with cousins, and aunts, and uncles that I was not able to form. I've sat in the pain and allowed God to carry me through to a place of healing. I acknowledged a hurt stemming from the deception and the desire to have experienced more father-daughter moments or wishing the relationship was better than it was, or wanting more time with him. But, I find comfort in knowing and trusting that God's plan and what He allowed was best.

If asked what advice I would have given my young mother if she had come to me, I would have encouraged my mother to be honest and transparent about the affair. I would have encouraged her to share the truth about her past with her daughter. People will pass judgment regardless if you hide the truth or live a lie, so **LIVE YOUR TRUTH.** If asked what I would say to the married unfaithful preacher, my advice would've been exactly the same.

For my sisters who share a similar story as mine, concerning their father, please know that avoiding the void can cause you pain. That ignored pain may cause you mistakes that can create more pain or friction in your relationships with men, your children, and their relationship with their father. So my sister, go ahead and acknowledge the void so that your hurt is not hurting others and so you can walk into your full purpose and worth! Acknowledge the void so you can heal from any of the hurt that it caused. Sis, don't allow the judgmental people in a church, your family, community, job or anywhere, make you second-guess God's love for you or your worth. I'm asking God to send you a tribe of **REAL** people who will love and support you through your shortcomings. I am asking Him to give you strength to acknowledge the void.

I tend to be more compassionate towards people because of my experiences. I had a baby out of wedlock shortly after announcing to the church that I was called to ministry. Throughout my entire pregnancy, I beat myself up and felt condemned. As soon as my daughter was born, I was set free from feelings of shame and guilt! Sis, God can do the same for you, too. I knew my daughter was conceived and born with purpose, and so were you! It doesn't matter what void you feel! Whether you know your biological parents, you're searching for the truth, or simply don't have the relationships you desire, just know that God loves you and He can fill the void. My story reminds me that people are human. We make mistakes and don't always make the best decisions. But even when we do we need compassion, grace, and unconditional love. Sister, I extend that same compassion and grace, and love to you. Take some for yourself as you acknowledge the void and live in your truth without guilt or shame. You are loved, valued, and worth it. God's love can fill the void.

THE INVISIBLE ME
By: Lenora Jones Elliott

"Children should be seen and not heard", this is a direct quote from my grandmother who I called Big Mama. This was truly her philosophy. Big Mama was the Matriarch of the household that I grew up in. So, needless to say, this was my foundation. I learned very early in life that

Silence = Safety! Being silent allowed me to slip below the radar... undetected. It kept me out of trouble, kept my name from being in the middle of stuff. I learned the silence really is golden!

I also learned (subconsciously) that my voice held no value and that my opinion was not important.

This was also a part of my foundation. I had no idea that it would set the stage for so many issues in life later on like low self-esteem, insecurities and even acute depression.

I am from very humble beginnings. My family didn't have a lot of money and now that I think about it... because of this, operating in survivor mode was my norm. Because we didn't have a lot of resources, I didn't dress like everyone else, I didn't have the things most of my peers were blessed with.

Because I didn't have a lot I knew not to draw attention to myself so I wouldn't get teased. I realized early in life that if nobody notices me, then they wouldn't pick on me. I became so good at the "invisible me" game, at some point even the teachers overlooked me on a regular basis. My silence kept me out of sight...thus out of mind!

As I grew into adulthood I realize (now) that I gravitated towards jobs where my lines were scripted. If I had a pre-approved script, I was fine. I looked for positions where I would not be expected to interact with others or forced to have a discussion where I had to rely on my own words.

I also surrounded myself with people who were outgoing and extroverts. This allowed me to come along for the ride without having to step outside my comfort zone. I was truly content allowing them to shine.

In May 1988, at the age of 18, while a freshman in college, I was assaulted by a stranger. I had seen him before, but I didn't know his name.

Nobody knew of this assault except one person. When I disclosed what happened. She told me to do 3 things – 1. Go to the hospital to get examined 2. Take my Final Exams 3. Leave school and go home!

I sat with those instructions for a minute....and I realized that if I went to the hospital I would have to disclose what happened to me. What if they made me report it...who would believe me?

So I made the decision to go to the clinic on campus instead.

I told them some of the details about the experience. They must have believed me because they gave me medication instead of counseling and sent me home. At that time....in my mind.... My silence allowed me to escape an ordeal that I just wasn't ready to deal with. But how many of you know that I wasn't escaping at all! This allowed me to continue building walls around me to keep me safe. Those walls allowed me to become more invisible with each episode, each event, each decision in my life.

Over the next few years, I gained weight.... ALOT of weight. It was gradual, so I didn't realize that I had slipped into survivor mode. Subconsciously, my message to myself was, "If I am unattractive, NOBODY will pay any attention to me!" If they didn't see me, they couldn't hurt me.

I recently acknowledged that even in choosing a mate, I was drawn to the person whose personality, whose stature, whose presence was larger than mine. Not overly commanding to the point of making me uncomfortable, but large enough to allow me entrance into his reality...entrance into the world that he created and still remain unnoticed.

Often that person had automatic acceptance into certain arenas/groups because of who he was or what he had to offer. I was allowed entrance into that world only because I was with him. Not much was ever required of me....but in return not much was ever given to me either – like respect or opportunities for my voice to be heard.

This happened so much that most of the time I wasn't even addressed by my name...I have been referred to as Eleanore, Lorraine, Elaine, Leona (and the list goes on). I often had to say, my name is Lenora... and sometime I had to spell it out for them.... L-E-N-O-R-A!!!

I had to come to grips with the fact that this was the reality I created for myself through my silence.

I joined a ministry that I had been visiting for over a year. Before I joined the ministry one of the Pastors spoke to me and said, "Lenora, God says it is time for you to stop hiding." I was thinking....WHAT??? At first (I must admit) I was feeling some type of way, because in my mind, I wasn't hiding at all. So, I didn't think that word was for me so I didn't move.

She spoke to me again a few weeks later and said, "Lenora, this is your season to come out – to come forth". Hmmm...come out of what, is what I was thinking. No need to come out if I'm not hiding, so I didn't move.

The last message she gave me was so powerful that I actually felt a PUSH. She spoke to me about my season, what God was doing in my life, and she prayed for a covering over me. Then...she took my hand and started walking with me. She walked me across the altar. We walked from wall to wall. She was literally showing me that I had the strength to step out. She was showing me that I would not be alone once I stepped out and that there are assignments that I am responsible for, assignments that I must complete, charges that I haven't fulfilled and things that I cannot accomplish until I step forward.

Stepping forward requires Motion in the natural as well as in the spiritual.

Faith is an ACTION word and right now I am being called to do more, to be active and to come forth.

I will admit that this move is big for me because I've remained in the same posture for years. I would do just enough to be active, but not enough to advance.

I would do just enough, so that I wouldn't totally disappear, but not enough to be visible. I'd do enough to be present but not enough to have a Presence.

"To who much is given, much is required."

It was then that I realized that I have to become Visible so that others can see God through me.

So, to my sisters who find themselves in hiding...those who are blending into the crowd or allowing the walls to absorb them...to you I say...I AM YOU....This was my life. God called me forth to be used for His Glory. And if He found me worthy, believe me; He CAN do the same for you. In the words of Tye Tribett – "If He did it before, He can do it again."

Believe me, what He is doing with my life is only a fraction of what is in store for you.

Just Keep Moving Until You Are the Visible YOU!

YOU ARE NOT ALONE!

LETTERS TO MY SISTERS was carefully crafted for women who have experienced grief, loss, betrayal, and disappointment from childhood through adulthood. We've also created this community of storytellers to engage with a beautiful soul such as yourself by celebrating the reality that **YOU ARE NOT ALONE.**

Were you able to identify with any of the stories in this book? What do you know about yourself now that you didn't know before? The pain these fearless storytellers endured is quite heart-breaking, and the number of tears they have cried is immeasurable. The triumphant dimension they are now walking in is obtainable for any woman seeking comfort in her spirit, mind, body, and soul.

These brave women have **conquered various devastating circumstances** that could have cost them their lives. Instead of lying down in defeat, they decided to rise above the pain and embrace healing along with accountability through the art of storytelling. Even though they have told their stories, they are still on an amazing path to healing.

Over the next few days, **consider writing a letter to each of your sister-friends.** If you don't have friends to write to, feel free to write to us at fearlessstorytellers@gmail.com As you pour your heart out in your letter, you may feel like crying and may even feel anger or possibly shame. Feelings are temporary catalysts, and eventually, they will subside, but you must allow yourself to go through the pain to access true healing. We must take better care of our hearts or we will die in our pain and drown in our tears. Let's continue to triumph over our past and become the fearless women we were perfectly designed to be!

Adrienne E. Bell,
The Fearless Storytellers Movement, Founder & CEO

MY REFLECTIONS...

MY REFLECTIONS...

MY REFLECTIONS...

MY REFLECTIONS...

MY REFLECTIONS...

MY REFLECTIONS...

MY REFLECTIONS...

MY REFLECTIONS...

MY REFLECTIONS...

MY REFLECTIONS...

MY REFLECTIONS...

MY REFLECTIONS...

MY REFLECTIONS...

WHAT IS THE FEARLESS STORYTELLERS MOVEMENT?

For generations, women have been muzzled and threatened to speak their truth at the expense of losing their jobs, homes, marriages, and most importantly, their dignity. My heart BLEEDS at the amount of pain we, as women, have ALLOWED ourselves to participate in for the sake of "Love." I am taking the lead on removing that muzzle and empowering women to speak their truth with dignity and grace. The Fearless Storytellers Movement was created to tell the stories of courageous women and their journey to discover their self-worth.

When I shared this movement on social media in August of 2018, I had no idea what was in store for me. I am committed to gathering a tribe of women committed to learning from each other's mistakes and win the RIGHT way in our romantic, platonic, and familial relationships!

THE FEARLESS STORYTELLERS MOVEMENT is an invitation to look deeper into the souls of women who endured and overcame tremendous amounts of pain, disappointment, and betrayal. These culture-shifting stories are real, raw, and relatable. I trust you have found healing in at least ONE of these stories, and if you haven't, you know someone who would.

We trust you are **ENERGIZED, ENCOURAGED**, and **EMPOWERED** as you've experienced the heart-wrenching stories of courageous women bravely overcoming unimaginable circumstances.

Do you have a story to tell? The Fearless Storytellers would love to partner with you to share your story of triumph! We are searching for fearless storytellers unafraid to invest their time, talent, treasure, and

WHAT IS THE FEARLESS STORYTELLERS MOVEMENT?

testimony into this movement. We are looking for individuals who have endured the pain and ready to share how they have overcome trauma in the following areas:

- molestation or rape
- being a product of rape (father is known or unknown)
- being a product of incest
- have been married three or more times
- have struggled with infertility and have overcome
- were/are married to a man/woman in ministry and was cheated on with a member of the church
- in lesbian/gay/bisexual relationships before heterosexual marriage
- former swingers
- former ministry leaders/pastors who cheated on their husbands/wives
- are/have raised their husband's/wife's love child (ren) as their own
- were in a sexless marriage (husband is/was impotent or wife had no desire to engage in physical intimacy)
- husbands raped/molested their biological children or a family member

Every day, individuals are joining The Fearless Storytellers Movement. If you or someone you know wants to become an Official Fearless Storyteller, email fearlessstorytellers@gmail.com, whether single, married, divorced, separated or widowed, The Fearless. Storytellers Movement would LOVE to partner with you! (Men are welcome, too!) If your experience is not listed above, that's perfectly fine; we'd still love to hear your story for consideration in a later publication.

The muzzle has been removed...**LET THE FEARLESS STORYTELLING CONTINUE!**

WHAT IS THE FEARLESS STORYTELLERS MOVEMENT?

Adrienne E. Bell is the Founder of The Fearless Storytellers Movement specializing in helping women remove the proverbial muzzle and tell their story their way. As a Culture-Shifting Problem Solver and Storyteller, Adrienne's unique purpose is to empower humanity to achieve excellence in business, love, and life.

Made in the USA
Columbia, SC
16 June 2025